MW00770948

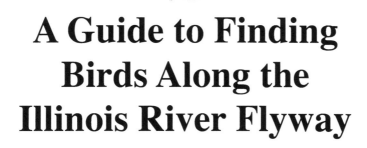

A Guide to Finding Birds Along the Illinois River Flyway

Joe Steensma
Colin Dobson

SHEBA Media

St. Louis, Missouri

Copyright © 2018 by Joseph T. Steensma

All rights reserved. No part of this publication may be reproduced, distributed, or transmitted in any form or by any means, without prior writ-ten permission.

Grace Rae Holdings, LLC dba SHEBA Media
12760 Corum Way Drive
St. Louis, Missouri

A Guide to Finding Birds Along the Illinois River Flyway
Joseph T. Steensma
ISBN 978-0-9886382-2-8

ACKNOWLEDGEMENTS

To my grandparents and parents and sister, through whom I have learned so much. Their love, support, and guidance has given me the confidence to chase my dreams…and birds.
— *Colin*

To Kristie, who has tolerated 27 years of me showing up late and muddy after countless days hours of chasing birds. I would also like to thank my children Nate, Grace, and Zeke for being the best spotters a dad could hope for.
— *Joe*

We would also like to thank Lydia Duran for the design and layout of the book, Aishwarya Nagar for mapping locations, and Eliza Dent for research conducted for this project.

TABLE OF CONTENTS

PREFACE

A few years ago an interactive game called Pokèmon© GO exploded on to the market. The idea is that one could use one's smart phone to navigate to an actual place (in the real world) and 'catch' creatures, called Pokemon, from the virtual world. I was in Australia at the time of the game's release. I was birding ('bird' is a verb, as in "Hey, do you wanna bird today"?) at a park in the city of Wollongong where I saw throngs of young people swarming the park looking at trees, holding smart phones in the air. Like any birder, I was curious as to what they might have found, so I went to a group and asked "What are you looking at?", expecting them to say "We found a Blue-Winged Kookaburra" or something. They responded "There is a Pikachu around here". Now, I don't purport to be an expert when it comes to Australian birds, but I was fairly certain that "Pikachu" was not an avian species. Still, I looked at the tree, wherein I found a Powerful Owl (a giant raptor, whose primary prey are the massive 'flying fox' bats found in Australia). I proceeded to have a full-on 'bird-gasm'. I was ecstatic and was (quite literally) jumping around as if I had won the lottery. The kids around me sensed my excitement and came running over, perhaps hoping that they could score a 'Pikachu' or some other virtual creature. At first they were clearly disappointed when I told them that I had found an *actual, living creature,* but once I trained my spotting scope on the owl and the first brave souls stepped up to take a look, the jaws began to drop. Kid after kid waited in line to see the bird, which seemed all too happy to appease their curiosity. In all, no less than 30 kids were able to see this most amazing species. More importantly, I was able to explain to them that these 'actual, living creatures' were more ubiquitous and more interesting than any 'virtual' creature they could be hoping to spot in the exact same tree. I know, unequivocally, that several 'birders' were 'hatched' that day. For me, that experience underscored the reason why birdwatching has been the fastest growing hobby in the United States over the past 20 years. It is one of those rare activities that brings people together in ways that few other activities can. Young and old. Hippies and corporate executives. Republicans and Democrats. We might all come from different places or be at different places in our lives, but when we look upon a beautiful bird we are all struck with a sense of awe. Birdwatching compels us to be what our species was made to be; collaborators...explores...adventurers...discoverers. It has the unique ability to connect us to our environment, but more importantly birdwatching connects us to each other in ways that few activities can. This ability...to connect people...is what we love about birdwatching and why we wrote this book. Our hope is that we might convince more people to go out and explore, and connect to one another.

While birdwatching can be a lot of things (adventurous, relaxing, competitive, collaborative) one thing it will always be is FUN. If you are birding and not having fun, you are either doing it wrong or with the wrong people. To help you in your birding career we have a few rules that we feel are pretty important to share.

Rule #1: Don't birdwatch with jerks.

If a person is a jerk when he is not bird-watching, he will very likely be a jerk when he is birdwatching. There more sub-species of 'jerks' in the world than there are birds, but our worst-tolerated sub-species are the 'whiner' (*Homo sapiens complainerensus*) and the 'shouter' (*Homo sapiens loudmoutherus*). You may have your own worst tolerated species. If so, limit your exposure to them so as to avoid 'jerkanitus', a condition that can keep you out of birding for extended periods.

Rule #2: Don't be a know-it-all.

Look, we have all known those people who "know everything" about whatever their passion is. You know the type—the "been-there, done-that" person who is a total buzz kill. Those people fall squarely into the "jerk" category. You DO NOT WANT TO FALL IN THAT CATEGORY (See rule #1)!

Rule #3: Don't be a buzz kill.

We have birded (again, birded is a the past tense of the verb form of 'bird') thousands of times at the locations described in this book still get jazzed about seeing all types of birds that we have seen thousands of times (though Colin is not a huge fan of House Sparrows). Truthfully, no one enjoys bird watching with people who say things like, "Oh, we saw that bird yesterday" or "That bird is boring."

The point is, no bird deserves to be written off as "common" or "just a(n) [fill in the blank]." How would you like it if the a bird who was watching you said, "Oh, it's just another female human," or "It's just another rude American."? That doesn't feel very good, does it? Well, birds have feelings, too. Don't write off a bird just because it isn't super sexy. Maybe it has a cool personality or lives in some pretty terrific place. Maybe it is an amazing singer or has some crazy behaviors. Just remember you are an individual, and so is each of the birds you will be looking at. Nobody, including birds, likes hanging out with judgmental people.

Rule #4: Everything is a game.

For us, birding is not just some leisure activity; it is a chance for adventure, competition, and amazing shared experiences. We strongly encourage you to create small challenges or games while birding.

We have what we call "burger birds." A list of burger birds is established before the spotting begins. Usually (at least for us), the list contains birds we really want to see or one that is special to us for some reason (e.g., it rescued us from a burning building when we were infants). When someone spots a burger bird, the rest of the team buys that person burger (or whatever) after the day is done and you are recounting the best parts of your 'birdventure'.

Also, if you are not too fond of the name of any bird, go ahead and give it a new name. We have dubbed the Painted Bunting "P-Bizzle," not because we dislike the name "Painted Bunting" but because we felt it was too much of a bad-ass not to have a nickname. The point is not to take it too seriously. We often challenge ourselves to see particular species or a certain number of species, but not at the expense of having fun.

Rule #5: Don't Over-plan.

Actually, this is a relatively common sub-species of jerk; the over-planner (*Homo sapiens analretentivus*). Even if you are not an over-planner, be careful not to be too prescriptive about what your birding adventure will look like. Sometimes places where you plan to spend relatively little time end up being amazing and compel you to spend more time. Other times hotspots are really not that hot. Be flexible. Within this guide we have tried to provide lots of different places with a lot of different types of habitats. Not every one of these will be popping with birds at the same time. Try to plan your day around a few places, but leave yourself plenty of room to adjust…and maybe even find your own hotspot along the way.

Rule #6: Respect ... everything.

You might have surmised that Colin and Joe are always willing to clown around while bird-watching. We honestly believe that bird-watching is a celebration of creation. But just because we have a blast every time we bird, doesn't mean we are disrespectful. Quite the contrary, we deeply respect the property, people, and creatures (of all types) we encounter while we are birding.

The people of Central Illinois are amazingly kind and friendly, but don't be a jerk and go onto property to watch birds without permission. The birds of the region are awesome, but don't plow through a patch skunk cabbage (ignoring its beauty and disrespecting the habitat) to see a bird.

The point: Respect the dignity of all people, places, and creatures while you are having a ball bird-watching.

Rule #7: Share the love.

You may have figured this out already; we are on a mission, and we need your help. Our mission is to spread the Gospel of Birds. If you are coming to our region to birdwatch consider packing an extra set of binoculars to leave at a school or an extra field guide (maybe even this one!) to give to a kid you meet. Or maybe consider giving a donation to the parks you visit. Even doing something as simple as inviting people to look through your spotting scope or go birding with you can make a huge difference in a person's day or how they connect with their environment.

We believe that the more people who see the amazing diversity and complete awesomeness of the bird life we have throughout Central Illinois, the more likely that people will advocate for protection of habitat and for policies that protect our environment.

Organization and Structure

This is not an identification guide. The purpose of this guide is to help the user find birds along the Illinois River Flyway and the habitats that are ideal for certain species of birds. This guide is intended for use as a companion guide to any field guide to North American birds you can get your hands on. That said, we do recommend that you get a field guide that encompasses "North American" birds, as opposed to birds of the "Eastern United States". The reason is because there are many species that are not commonly found in the "Eastern US", that can be reported in this region. There are also a number of apps for smart phones that excellent resources as well.

This book describes the best places to find approximately 320 species that we have spotted in the region. While this is a lot of species, our intent is not to provide a comprehensive listing of every bird one could possibly see in the region. It is also not exhaustive in terms of the habitats included in the text. In fact, there are hundreds of specific locations for which we have documented detailed species records, but they are not all included in this book. We are not trying to cheat the reader and save all of the best spots for ourselves (though the thought did cross our minds). Rather, we want to focus on the most productive birding locations in the region so that, if you are new to birding or new to the region, you can have a great birding experience on your first trip.

We have found many of these spots through years of exploration. While we hope this guide gives you a distinct advantage in your birdwatching adventures along the Illinois River flyway, we also encourage everyone to explore the area and find your own "secret hotspots," just as we have done through the years.

ALL BIRDING HOTSPOTS

1. Anderson Lake (page 28)
2. Areas South of Havana (page 29)
3. Banner Marsh (page 32)
4. Batchtown (page 34)
5. Beardstown Marsh and Arenz Road (page 35)
6. Big Lake (page 37)
7. Chautauqua NWR (page 39)
8. Columbia Bottom State Conservation Area (page 43)
9. Copperhead Hollow (page 47)
10. Double T (page 49)
11. East St. Louis Area (page 51)
12. Emiquon NWR (page 54)
13. Jim Edgar Panther Creek (page 59)
14. Meredosia Area (page 61)
15. Peoria Lake (page 66)
16. Pere Marquette State Park (page 68)
17. Riverlands, Big Muddy NWR (Cora Island Unit), Ted and Pat Jones State Park (page 71)
18. Sand Ridge State Forest (page 78)
19. Sanganois and Surrounding Areas (page 81)
20. Siloam Springs State Park (page 84)
21. Spring Lake (page 89)
22. Spunky Bottoms and Farmland (page 91)
23. Stump Lake and Surrounding Areas (page 93)
24. Two Rivers - Swan Lake and Pohlman Slough (page 96)

12

NORTHERN BIRDING HOTSPOTS

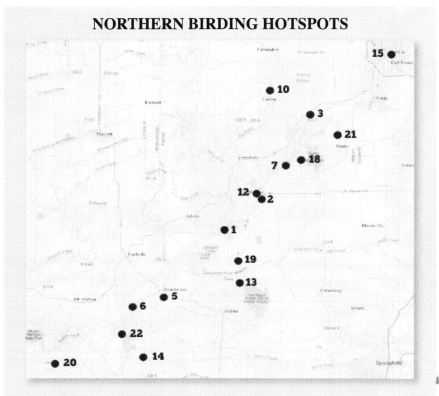

1. Anderson Lake (page 28)
2. Areas South of Havana (page 29)
3. Banner Marsh (page 32)
5. Beardstown Marsh and Arenz Road (page 35)
6. Big Lake (page 37)
7. Chautauqua NWR (page 39)
10. Double T (page 49)
12. Emiquon NWR (page 54)
13. Jim Edgar Panther Creek (page 59)
14. Meredosia Area (page 61)
15. Peoria Lake (page 66)
18. Sand Ridge State Forest (page 78)
19. Sanganois and Surrounding Areas (page 81)
20. Siloam Springs State Park (page 84)
21. Spring Lake (page 89)
22. Spunky Bottoms and Farmland (page 91)

SOUTHERN BIRDING HOTSPOTS

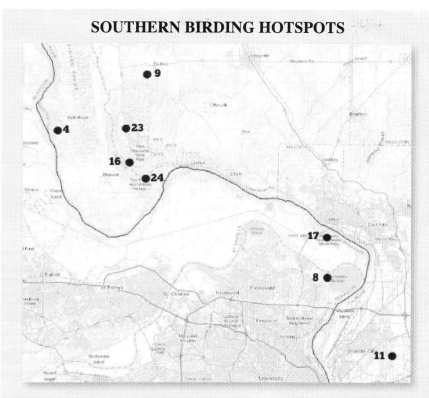

CHAPTER ONE:
A PRIMER ON THE REGION

Let's get this out of the way first: We are fully aware of the fact that when most people think of "North American Birding Hotspots" Central Illinois is not front of mind. We get it…and we are not (greatly) offended if you are skeptical of our claim that this area is one of the best places in the United States to birdwatch. The truth is that birding has long been overshadowed by Honest Abe. Let's face it, Central Illinois has been riding that "Land of Lincoln" gravy train for the past 150 years. It's been a good gig, but we believe it is high-time the world know about the vast diversity of species and habitats that exist in this relatively small area.

There are a few reasons why this area is so productive, but the most important one is water; more specifically, the Illinois and Mississippi Rivers. These are the 'super-highways' that birds follow when they migrate (or, in the case of wayward vagrants, stick to when they are lost). The rivers and their associated floodplains provide ample food and cover for millions of migrating and nesting birds throughout the year.

The Mississippi River flyway is one of the best known flyways in the world. Birdwatchers from around the globe visit the flyway at its southern-most point (near New Orleans) during the fall-outs of spring migration. This is, without question, an ornithological wonder. After traveling hundreds, even thousands, of miles these little birds come to Mississippi River Delta physically exhausted. It is here that the birds make a pitstop before the make their way north, to their breeding grounds. The Mississippi River is their highway to 'home' so to speak, and the banks, floodplains, marshes, and forests along the way are 'feeding troughs' for these intrepid travelers.

The Illinois River

About 25 miles north of St. Louis, Missouri the Illinois River joins the Mississippi River, and about 20 miles south is the confluence of the Mississippi and Missouri Rivers. While the Mississippi and Missouri Rivers are more well-known, the Illinois River is a consequential waterway in its own right. It drains nearly 30,000 sq. miles from southwestern Michigan, to Wisconsin, through most of central Illinois. What makes the Illinois River Flyway so unique is that it has a diverse set of habitats that not only accommodate the migrating species, but also provides excellent habitat for nesting (breeding) species as well. In fact, the number of nesting species in such a small area is really quite impressive. But that is not all that makes it special. Many migrating birds will use the Illinois River as the 'highway' to the Great Lakes. While some migrating birds will continue north along the Mississippi, or head west on the Missouri, a large number of birds will head northeast along the Illinois River to Lake Michigan and their breeding grounds to the north. Add in the fact that the region sees a disproportionate number of vagrant or 'accidental' species, and it becomes clear why we believe you would be hard pressed to find many places in the Continental US that offer the accessibility to birds and the variety of species that can be found in the Illinois River Flyway. To paraphrase Forrest Gump, with the variety of habitats and seasons, when it comes to birding the Illinois River is "like a box of chocolates…you never know what you are going to get".

Seasons

While we recognize many readers will be familiar with Illinois (and the climate therein), we hope that at least some readers will be from faraway places and may not be as familiar with Illinois and its (famously temperamental) weather and seasons. The Illinois River Flyway experiences four distinct seasons, each one of them provides different climates and distinct birdwatching opportunities.

The winter months span from December to late March. Winters can, at times, be very cold. Temperatures below 0 degrees Fahrenheit are frequently recorded and snow is a very real possibility from November through March. Add in a consistent bone-chilling wind and it is understandable why one might say "I think I will wait for spring". Our advice is that you don't make that mistake! Ironically, in spite of the cold temperatures, this is our favorite time of year to explore this area. While one is not likely to see the numbers of species one might see on a typical spring day, the wandering vagrants and hobos of the wind seem to find their way to Central Illinois throughout the winter and, more specifically, find their way to many of the locations detailed in this book. The objective truth is that winter birding in this region can be amazing, even if the numbers of species seen on any given day is not. Each day is a chance at a 'once-in-a-lifetime' find. Jaegers, Scoters,

Long-tailed ducks, California Gulls, and any number of wayward passerines turn up each year. In fact, we have noted an uptick in oddities (vagrants, as they are known in the ornithological vernacular) across the region over the past several years. While the scientific community has not settled on an exact reason as to why this is the case, it is undeniable that climate change and increasingly mild winters have changed the behavior of birds significantly over the past decade or so. As more citizen-scientists (like you!) engage in birdwatching and report their sightings, particularly in the winter months, we can better understand the changing behaviors of birds and the effects of a changing climate on them.

A word of caution for the intrepid souls that venture out into the winter cold: Any birdwatching adventure planned for winter should have contingencies for cold temperatures and frozen precipitation (ice and/or snow). Many of the locations detailed in this book are rural and susceptible to poor road conditions, especially in snowy or icy conditions. Check the weather and plan your trip accordingly.

Signs of spring emerge in Central Illinois in the month of March. Waterfowl and shorebirds start showing up first and the rains that define "springtime" in Illinois arrive not long thereafter. The rains turn floodplains into shallow feeding troughs for the shorebirds, wading birds, and waterfowl that pour through the flyway on their way to their breeding grounds. As temperatures rise and sprigs of green emerge the forests, fields, marshes, and prairies come to life. To be clear, springtime is truly spectacular for birdwatching along the Illinois River, with April and May being mind-blowingly good. Spring migration is like a season-long fireworks show; it starts with waterfowl and shorebirds, but ends in grand fashion with wave after wave of colorful migrant and nesting songbirds. Their songs echoing through the forests and fields in an almost dizzying symphony. Having bird watched all over the world we are often asked "What is the best place you have ever birdwatched"? Of course, there are lots of factors that go into making such a determination, but a good spring day on the Illinois River Flyway has to be in the Top 10. It is not unusual to log 150 species on a spring day in the region. More importantly, especially for the person who is not from the area, or is otherwise new to North American birds, is that the habitats and environs highlighted in this book provide for really great views of birds. In fact, we often tell people who have never been to North America that if you can only birdwatch in one place in the US, this may be the place…and springtime is definitely the time. Sure, there are places that might produce more species…and possibly more individual birds…but what makes this region so remarkable (especially in spring) is that one can see birds that are typically found west of the Mississippi River…and birds that are found east. One can see birds that breed in the Arctic…and birds that are considered "southern" breeders. While there are not many regional endemics (or 'specialties', so to speak) in the area (especially compared to areas like Southeast Arizona, for example), the springtime offers a cross-section of North American species that represent more genera than any other gathering of birds in the continental US…and the weather is often beautiful as well.

As the weather warms and the migrants head north, summer sets in. From St. Louis to Peoria summers along the Illinois River can be described in one word: HUMID! While June can be mild and not overly oppressive, July quickly reminds us why we love spring. And August? Well, let's just say that if it weren't for the prospect of early shorebirds, we would have very likely taken up an indoor hobby by now. In all seriousness, summers are for nesting along the Illinois River and there are many breeding birds that nest in the region. There is no question that the birding is more difficult in the summer than it is in the spring or winter. The trees have leaves, the reeds and cattails have overtaken ponds and wetlands, the prairie grasses that were nonexistent just weeks prior are now several feet tall, and the open fields of winter and spring are chockfull of crops. But do not despair! There is good birdwatching throughout the region, even if it takes a little more work…and patience. The birds will be more reclusive, especially after they have nested, but they are around and some of the species that are found are quite rare indeed! The region has a number of birds that "aren't supposed to breed here." Apparently, the Scissor-Tailed Flycatchers, Bewick's Wrens, Painted Buntings and many others species we have observed nesting at the locations detailed herein, don't read field guides. If they did, they would clearly see that they are not supposed to be here! In fact, the area has garnered some measure of fame in the birdwatching community for being able to attract nesting birds that would be considered 'out of range.' So, even in the dog-days of summer, the birding can be excellent and well worth the time.

By August the (less organized) fall migration begins to roll through the region. Shorebirds meandering through, on their way south (some of which actually arrive as early as July), remind us that the seasons will change and that the seemingly incessant heat and humidity of summer will give way to autumn. By late September birds of all sorts amble through the region on their way south. Some of them hustle through quickly, while others stay for a spell. Still others, like the Snow Geese and Trumpeter Swans, stay through the winter. The dynamics of spring and fall migration are kind of like "Happy Hour" at a bar. The specials start at 5 PM and throngs of people flock in at exactly 5 PM. The time at which people leave is an entirely different story. Some leave right at 6 PM, while others stick around for another round. Then there are those who stay wayyyy too late. At any rate, people trickle out in a less predictable fashion than how they arrived. Spring migration can be thought of as the beginning of 'happy hour'. Every bird wants to get to the prime nesting site as soon as possible, so birds come through in a predictable fashion. They roll through, grab a snack, take a nap, and get back to the sky. Fall migration is a little less predictable, and (it could be argued) a little more interesting. There are a lot more variables that might impact when birds arrive to the region in the fall, but just like the revelers at the bar, everyone leaves at some point...some just much later than others. For this reason, fall is a season that has the certainty of migration, with the unpredictability associated with people who drank too much at happy hour. And for many of the same reasons you might want to sit outside a bar and watch people as they leave, we love to go bird watching in the fall along the Illinois River. Sometimes you will see birds, like a Cinnamon Teal, hanging out with a Gadwall and you can imagine the thoughts going through its head: "Oh man! I left with HIM?!?! I should have gone home with Paul! Why did I stay? The band was not even that good! Man-oh-man, do I have a headache". In all seriousness, there are a lot locations we have highlighted that are simply exceptional hotspots for fall birdwatching, but the primary variables in most of those locations is water and mudflats! After all the thousands and thousands of hours we have spent in the field chasing fall migrants, those attributes, more than any other, determine the abundance and longevity of stay for fall migrants, at least in terms of shorebirds and ducks. Passerines and birds of prey that migrate through are less dependent on those conditions, and therefore a little more predictable overall, but still less predictable than what they were just a few months before.

The truth is that each season offers a unique birdwatching opportunity. Whether you are a seasoned veteran or a newly 'fledged' birder you are very likely to find something you have never seen before along the Illinois River.

Habitats

It is estimated Illinois has lost over 90% of its wild habitats since Honest Abe left Springfield for Washington DC. To be clear, we are not saying his departure caused this devastating loss of habitat...but we aren't saying it DID NOT cause it either! In all seriousness, the prairies, forests, and wetlands that used to dominate the landscape of Illinois are mere remnants of what they once were, and this has had a profound impact on the birdlife within the state. Fortunately, there have been great efforts to restore, preserve, and protect the remaining fragments of habitats and much of those efforts have been focused along the Illinois River Flyway. Because of these efforts there are, quite literally, dozens of fantastic properties that provide critical habitat to breeding, migrant, and over-wintering birds.

There are several types of plant communities that can be found in the Illinois River Flyway. Each habitat is distinguished by characteristic plants, animals, and physical attributes. We have no desire to delve into the minutia of each of these biological communities, but we do believe it is important to know the types of habitats that can be found in the region and the birds typically found therein. In the following chapter there are detailed descriptions of two dozen properties, many of which have multiple habitats, and (consequently) many species of birds that can be found. Other properties have only one type of habitat, but the habitat is rare or rather isolated, which can be great for 'hard to find species'. Either way, we felt it necessary to include 'dominant habitats' in the descriptions provided in Chapter 2, and therefore felt it important to at least introduce habitats here.

Forest and Woodland

Forests and woodlands are two different types of habitats that both have hardwood trees such as oaks, hickories, maples, and ash. The two are typically differentiated by the amount of understory vegetation and the amount of sunlight that makes it to the ground. Forests have a dense canopy, with significant understory, whereas woodlands have a more open canopy and relatively little understory growth. There are many properties highlighted in the book that have either one, or both of these habitats. Typical birds might include:

Cooper's Hawk, Sharp-shinned Hawk, Broad-winged Hawk, Whip-poor-will, Yellow-billed Cuckoo, Eastern Wood-pewee, White-eyed Vireo, Red-eyed Vireo, White-breasted Nuthatch, Gray Catbird, Northern Parula, Pine Warbler, Black-and-white Warbler, Kentucky Warbler, Scarlet Tanager, and Summer Tanager

Grassland and Prairie

The difference between these two habitats is not inconsequential for ecologists and botanists, but in terms of avifauna they are very similar. Just as there is "old growth forests" and "secondary forests" (where the former has never been logged or cleared and the latter has), prairies have never been tilled, whereas grasslands have. Because true prairie has never seen the plow, there are virtually no "true prairies" left in Illinois. In general, what is called tallgrass prairies in Illinois are open habitats of with sparse trees and shrubs...technically a grassland. As soon as a few trees emerge and provide any measure of cover the habitat would technically be called a savanna. Savanna is a transitional habitat. The terms grassland, prairie, and savanna are often used synonymously, though they are technically different. In this text we will use prairie and grassland synonymously, but will reserve savanna for areas that have woody plant growth. Prairies and grasslands are known for the incredible diversity of flowering plants that grow within them. This diversity plants is what allows for the great variety of the regions grassland-dependent species such as Henslow's Sparrow, Grasshopper Sparrow, Short-eared Owl, Upland Sandpiper, Northern Harrier, Bobolink, Dickcissel, Brown Thrasher, and Eastern Meadowlark.

Wetland/Marsh

Wetland habitats are characterized saturated soil dominated by hydrophilic (water-loving) plants. Many of the properties described in this book have large areas of wetlands, and much of the regions ecology is influenced by this habitat. Just like forests and grasslands, there are actually many types of wetlands, but the two that are found in the Illinois River flyway are ephemeral wetlands and emergent marshes. Ephemeral wetlands are those wetlands that are seasonal. They are very common in the region, but also transient and somewhat unpredictable. Emergent marshes are different in that they remain the same year after year and have persistent vegetation. These wetlands support a vast number of plants, birds, bats, insects, and other invertebrates. In terms of birdlife, the wetland habitats are perhaps the most productive in the region. Waterfowl, shorebirds, wading birds, swallows, wrens, and birds of prey can be found in abundance in these habitats.

Rivers and Lakes

So far we have kept things on the up-and-up when it comes to discussing habitats, but that all ends now. We fully expect to get hate-mail from ecologists and limnologists for what we are about to say. While we are fully aware that lakes and rivers are different, for the purposes of this book, we have lumped them together. We are classifying freshwater habitats that do not meet the criteria of a wetland as lakes. The truth is that the backwater sloughs of the Mississippi and Illinois Rivers are really not that different than lakes, at least in terms of birdlife. And what determines the types of birds found on a lake is not that different than what determines the types of birds found on a river. Unquestionably, large rivers (like the Illinois and Mississippi) are consequentially different than small rivers and streams, and we are not suggesting that those small rivers and streams be considered as lakes. That said, many of the lake habitats identified in this book are actually wide areas of the Illinois River and the birds found on the 'true lakes' described herein are not substantively different than those found on the large rivers. Birds such as Bank and Northern Rough-winged Swallows, all manners of ducks, loons, phalaropes, gulls, terns, Bald and Golden Eagles, Osprey, and even Jaegers are reported on the lakes (and rivers) in the region.

Agricultural/Mixed Use

Remember when we told you how Honest Abe took all the natural habitats with him when he left to save the Union (if not, see the opening paragraph on habitats above)? Well, those habitats were replaced with something. Sometimes it was cities, but more often than not they were replaced with agricultural land. Active agricultural land, old fields, peri-urban and sub-urban environments may not be "natural" habitats, but a wide-variety of birds frequent them nonetheless. Fallow farmland, which is fairly common throughout much of Central Illinois is in the early stage of reverting back to nature and can be excellent hotspots for songbirds and gamebirds. Wooded hedgerows are common in agricultural land and are often overgrown with Osage Orange, Honey/Black Locust, cherries, and wild rose. Active agricultural land can also be very productive for the keen birder, especially after harvest, when birds of all sorts forage for spilled or remnant grains. Northern Cardinal, Orchard Oriole, Lark Sparrow, Horned Lark, Lapland Longspur, Bobolink, Blue Grosbeak, Northern Mockingbird, Mourning Dove, Barn Swallow, Field Sparrow, American Tree Sparrow, Purple Finch, American Goldfinch, Purple Martin, and Northern Bobwhite are all commonly found in these habitats.

Now that you know what to expect from each season and each habitat, it is time to plan your trip. In the following chapters you will find all the information needed to begin your Illinois River birding adventure. Remember, we found many of the 'hotspots' we discuss later by simply stopping when we see good habitat. This guide is intended to be the beginning of a journey...not the end. We hope you add to it and make your own discoveries that advance our collective understanding of this important and incredible region.

CHAPTER TWO:
BIRDING HOT SPOTS

This chapter is intended to provide guidance to the possible locations of specific birds. Before we get into that, let's talk a little bit about how this chapter is organized. First, we note the difficulty of access to the site, as well as the recommended duration of an excursion, which does not include travel time. Also, each location has a table in which specific birds are listed. There are three categories: Should Find it Here, Might Find it Here, Unlikely to see it anywhere (but this is your best chance).

The first category, "Should Find it Here," points out birds that are found in relatively few places, but commonly found in the specified location. This category will not include ubiquitous birds, like the American Robin, Ring-Billed Gull, Morning Dove, and Turkey Vulture. In fact, these birds will not appear on any specific location list because they are so common that it does not make sense to include them on any one particular location list. The birds listed in this category are observed on more than 70 percent of birdwatching trips in this area, provided the season is the peak season for that species.

The second category, "Might Find it Here," consists of birds that are uncommon at a particular location, but are recorded at that location more frequently than at most other sights. The birds listed are observed on less than 50 percent, but more than 10 percent of bird-watching trips.

The last category, "Unlikely to See it Anywhere (but this is your best chance)," are the unicorns, the "lifers," the birds we have seen very rarely overall, but have recorded at a particular location.

In addition to the bird table, we have included a location description and GPS coordinates for specific hotspots or areas that we know to be particularly good for birding, based on the vegetative zone or specific features.

As stated previously, the targets listed at any location are not intended to represent a complete list of what can be seen at each location. For example, Columbia Bottom (a property near the confluence of Missouri and Mississippi Rivers) has relatively few "targets," but a good day at Columbia Bottom can easily yield seventy species.

Anderson Lake

Ease of access: Generally easy depending on water levels
Duration: around a half hour depending on shorebird numbers
Dominant habitat: Lake and forest

Should find it here	
	Common Merganser (W)
	American-white Pelican (Sp, Su, F)
	Osprey (Sp, Su, F)
	Bald Eagle (All)
	Semipalmated Plover (Sp & F)
	Semipalmated Sandpiper (Sp & F)
	Dunlin (Sp & F)
	Stilt Sandpiper (Sp & F)
	Short-billed Dowitcher (Sp & F)

	Purple Martin (Sp, Su, F)
Might find it here	
	Greater Scaup (W)
	Sanderling (F)
	Baird's Sandpiper (Sp & F)
	Buff-breasted Sandpiper (F)
	Wilson's Phalarope (Sp & F)
	Franklin's Gull (Sp & F)

Anderson Lake is a state property located in Southeastern Fulton county. Best times to bird here are in the spring and early fall, as this area is heavily hunted during the late fall months.

Turn east onto N Anderson Lake Drive off of Highway 100. Purple Martins and Eurasian-tree Sparrows are usually seen at the entrance of Anderson Lake. The lake itself is usually devoid of birds, but goldeneyes and mergansers can be seen during some cold winters and Ospreys can be seen during the summer.

Turn right when you go down to the boat ramp and continue on the road to the south. After passing some campers, you'll see the causeway, which heads east across the south end of Anderson Lake. Continue onto the causeway if the gate is open. The area south of the causeway is called Carlson Lake. In some years, this area can be low. If this is the case hundreds of ducks and shorebirds can be seen. Uncommon birds like Greater Scaup, Piping Plover, Marbled Godwit, and Buff-breasted Sandpiper have been seen. Also, all seven woodpecker species, Northern Parulas, and American Redstarts can be seen in the bottomland forests just east of Carlson Lake.

Areas South of Havana

Ease of Access: Generally easy
Duration: 1-2 hours
Dominant habitat: Agriculture and prairie

Should find it here	
	Northern Bobwhite (All)
	Semipalmated Sandpiper (Sp)
	Dunlin (Sp)
	Common Nighthawk (Sp & Su)
	Willow Flycatcher (Sp & Su)
	Western Kingbird (Sp & Su)
	Sedge Wren (Sp, Su, F)
	Northern Mockingbird (All)
	Yellow Warbler (Sp & Su)
	Lark Sparrow (Sp, Su, F)
	Grasshopper Sparrow (Sp & Su)
	Blue Grosbeak (Sp, Su, F)
	Bobolink (Sp & F)
Might find it here	
	Greater Scaup (W)
	Wild Turkey (All)
	Rough-legged Hawk (W)
	Semipalmated Plover (Sp & F)
	Sanderling (Sp & F)
	WIlson's Phalarope (Sp)
	Bell's Vireo (Sp & Su)
	Smith's Longspur (Sp)
	Yellow-breasted Chat (Sp & Su)
	Vesper Sparrow (All)
Unlikely to find it here (but this is your best bet)	
	Scissor-tailed Flycatcher (Sp & Su)
	Loggerhead Shrike (All?)

Although there are no preserves, the diverse "urbanized habitat" south of Havana will give birders chances to see some interesting birds that are hard to find in Central Illinois.

Start on 1550 E heading south out of Havana. You will eventually see the small cemetery on the east side of the road and the large "power plant pond" on the west, (40.280910, -90.065977). During the winter months, the power plant pond stays mostly open, which provides habitat for thousands of geese and ducks. All five goose species and Greater Scaup can be seen often. Long-tailed Ducks have been spotted in numbers in the past. During the spring and fall, look for shorebirds along the sandy edges in the northwest corner of the pond. Sanderlings and Ruddy Turnstones have been spotted at this location on more than one occasion. Also, the cemetery can be quite birdy during migration.

Continue south to the intersection with 1500 N. This intersection is your first chance to see Scissor-tailed Flycatcher and Western Kingbird, although not your best chance. One summer, a pair of Scissor-tailed Flycatchers were presumed unsuccessful with nesting at this location. This are is also a good area to see Vesper and Lark Sparrows. Turn east onto 1500 E and continue east.

After passing another intersection, there will be a large grassland to the south. This field is the best place to see Grasshopper Sparrows in the area. Also, Northern Mockingbird, Purple Martins, Blue Grosbeaks, Bobolinks, and Orchard Orioles can be seen often. A Loggerhead Shrike was seen here in the summer of 2016.

Continue over the railroad tracks and to the electrical substation on the northside of 1500 E. Take the second small gravel road to the north, and park here (40.275018, -90.045706). This area is the best area outside of East St. Louis to see a Western Kingbird in Illinois. Two to three pairs are regularly seen here during the summer, and have successfully bred several years in a row. Also, during some summers, a Scissor-tailed Flycatcher can be seen harassing the kingbirds. Northern Bobwhite, Northern Mockingbirds, Grasshopper and Vesper Sparrows, Blue Grosbeaks, and Eurasian-tree Sparrows can be seen here regularly. Lots of sparrows winter here and, during wet springs, Northern Waterthrushes can be seen as well.

Continue east past Highway 97. The field to the north is called "Sand Lake" (when it is flooded). Many uncommon birds have been seen here in wet springs. Six Eared Grebes were seen in a recent spring flooding, one pair stuck around and nested. Some uncommon shorebirds have been seen here (Wilson's and Red-necked Phalaropes), as well as some rare waders (Cattle Egrets, White-faced Ibis), and ducks (Cinnamon Teal). Also, listen for Smith's Longspurs in March and April.

Banner Marsh

Ease of access: Easy
Duration: 2-3 hours
Dominant habitat: Marsh and prairie

Should find it here	
	Mute Swan (All)
	Northern Bobwhite (All)
	Green Heron (Sp & Su)
	Osprey (Sp, Su, F)
	Willow Flycatcher (Sp, Su)
	Bell's Vireo (Sp, Su)
	Marsh Wren (All?)
	Yellow Warbler (Sp, Su, F)
	Orchard Oriole (Sp, Su, F)
	Eurasian-tree Sparrow (All)
Might find it here	
	Red-breasted Merganser (Sp)
	American Bittern (Sp & F)
	Least Bittern (Sp & Su)
	Cattle Egret (Sp & F)
	Short-eared Owl (W & Sp)
	Sedge Wren (Sp, Su, F)
	Henslow's Sparrow (Sp & Su)
	Grasshopper Sparrow (Sp, Su, F)
	Blue Grosbeak (Sp, Su, F)
	Bobolink (Sp & F)

Unlikely to find it here (but this is your best bet)	
	Northern Shrike (W)

Banner Marsh State Fish and Wildlife Area is located in Fulton and Peoria counties along the Illinois River. Managed primarily as a fishing property, it has many marshes and lakes that provide a great opportunity to see nesting marsh birds and migrating waterfowl.

There are three "parts" to Banner Marsh; Bell's Landing, Main Access, and East Access. It is our experience that Bell's Landing is the best out of the three, but all should be covered during the visit.

Start at Bell's Landing. To get here, take Highway 24 north from the small town of Banner, and take this for a few miles, you'll eventually reach the intersection with Marsh Road, (40.521426, -89.886975), which heads east. Turn east onto Marsh Road and continue east to the marsh and lakes throughout the south side of the Banner Marsh property. Explore the marshes and prairies in this area. Migrant waterfowl, nesting marsh birds like Least Bittern and Soras, and Ospreys, (most likely on the nesting platform towards the end of Marsh Road) can be seen here. One spring, a male Eurasian Wigeon was even seen here! Listen for Willow Flycatchers, Bell's Vireos, and Henslow's Sparrows during the summer and watch for a Northern Shrike during the winter around the prairies.

Continue back to Highway 24 and continue back north, before reaching the east access area, make a quick stop at the Main Access area, which is in between the two locations (40.537683, -89.862051). This is another area to locate birds like Least Bitterns and Willow Flycatchers.

After this, continue back north along Highway 24, and you'll reach the road for the East Access of Banner Marsh, Strube Road (40.550806, -89.833049). This is another area to see more marsh and prairie birds like Least Bitterns and Bell's Vireos, along with the chance to see some shorebirds, provided the water levels are optimal.

Batchtown

Ease of Access: Moderate, depends on water levels and walking distance
Duration: 1-3 hours
Dominant habitat: Forest and mudflat

Should find it here	
	American-white Pelican (Sp, Su, F)
	Bald Eagle (All)
	Least Sandpiper (Sp & F)
	Pileated Woodpecker (All)
	Northern Parula (Sp, Su, F)
	American Redstart (Sp, Su, F)
Might find it here	
	American Wigeon (Sp & F)
	Snowy Egret (Su & F)
	Little-blue Heron (Su & F)
	Osprey (Sp, Su, F)
	Mississippi Kite (Sp & Su)
	Black-necked Stilt (Sp, Su, F)
	Solitary Sandpiper (Sp & F)
	Semipalmated Sandpiper (Sp & F)
	Sanderling (Sp & F)
	Wilson's Phalarope (Sp & F)
	Least Tern (Sp, Su, F)
Unlikely to find it here (but this is your best bet)	
	Piping Plover (F)

Batchtown is a division of Two Rivers National Wildlife Refuge located in western Calhoun county along the Mississippi River, north of the Winfield Dam.

Batchtown is an interesting place as you have to plan your birding around the river level. About 1 mile south of Batchtown turn west into Smith Lane. If the river is low enough, continue on Smith Lane until you reach a small parking lot near the river (39.019797, -90.674925). At the small parking area listen for breeding species such as Eastern Wood Pewee, Great-crested Flycatcher, and American Redstart. Park here and walk out onto the dike.

The north area is a hunting club, but (in the right conditions) along the mudflats that form in this area one could see hundreds of shorebirds and ducks during spring and early fall. American Avocet and Black-necked Stilt have been seen here. Be sure to bring a spotting scope to check out the sandbars out on the Mississippi River. These sandbars are the only known successful Least Tern colony in West Central Illinois. Also, look for shorebirds on the sandbars as Piping Plover and Sanderling have been seen here. Be sure to also listen for Fish Crows and look for Bald Eagles, Ospreys, and Mississippi Kites.

Beardstown Marsh and Arenz Road

Ease of access: Easy
Duration: 2-3 Hours
Dominant habitat: Marsh and forest

Should find it here	
	Mute Swan (All)
	American Bittern (Sp & F)
	Least Bittern (Sp, Su, F)
	Green Heron (Sp, Su, F)
	Virginia Rail (All?)
	Sora (Sp, Su, F)
	Common Gallinule (Sp, Su, F)
	Whip-poor Will (Sp, Su, F)
	Marsh Wren (All?)

	Yellow Warbler (Sp & Su)
	Yellow-breasted Chat (Sp & Su)
	Lark Sparrow (Sp & Su)
	Grasshopper Sparrow (Sp & Su)
	Blue Grosbeak (Sp, Su, F)
Might find it here	
	Little-blue Heron (Su & F)
	Snowy Egret (Su & F)
	American Woodcock (Sp, Su, F)
	Chuck-wills-Widow (Sp, Su, F)
	Vesper Sparrow (All?)
Unlikely to find it here (but this is your best bet)	
	Black-bellied Whistling Duck (Su)
	King Rail (Sp & Su)
	Yellow-headed Blackbird (Sp & F)

Beardstown Marsh is a private property south of Beardstown, but can be seen from public roads. This is a large marsh that hosts many uncommon marsh breeders, which summer in Illinois. One could have a great afternoon of birding Beardstown Marsh!

Start from the intersection of Highway 100 and Boulevard Road and turn south onto Boulevard Road. You'll see Beardstown Marsh to the south of here. The north part of the property is the best place to see Mute Swans, ducks, Common Gallinules, and shorebirds. Black-bellied Whistling Ducks have been reported in recent summers. Continue to a gravel pull off along the road, (directly west from the Heritage Health Center.) Least Bitterns, Virginia Rails, Soras, Common Gallinules, Marsh Wrens, and Yellow Warblers can be seen from this pull-off.

The best area of the marsh is the area just south of the small ditch you cross over as you continue south on Boulevard Road. In the spring, many Virginia Rails can be seen in here. Also, listen for both bitterns, King Rails, Soras, and Marsh and Sedge Wrens.

During dry years, one might check the slough area along

Highway 67 south of Beardstown. Shorebirds and waders can be seen here in good numbers, with Western and Buff-breasted Sandpipers being seen here before. It should be said that there are not many pull-offs that provide good and safe viewing. Do not stop on the road to birdwatch. This is not only dangerous, but it also gives birders a bad name!

Also during summer months, Hagener Road west of Boulevard Road is the a good place to look for breeders. Lark, Vesper, and Grasshopper sparrows can be seen regularly . Northern Mockingbird and Blue Grosbeaks are common here as well.

Also if you're near Beardstown during a summer evening, check Arenz Road south of Highway 100, southeast of Beardstown. Besides the Siloam Springs area, this is the only other place in Central Illinois to see Chuck-wills-widow. The best spot is at the Junction of Arenz Road and Jeanieton Avenue, (39.985788, -90.378267). Also American Woodcocks, Whip-poor-wills, and Yellow-breasted Chat can be heard here as well.

Big Lake

Ease of Access: Hard, view from the road unless gate is open.
Duration: 2-3 hours
Dominant habitat: Lake and prairie

Should find it here	
	American-white Pelican (Sp, Su, F)
	Bald Eagle (All)
	Short-billed Dowitcher (Sp & F)
	American Pipit (Sp & F)
	Lincoln's Sparrow (Sp & F)
Might find it here	
	Golden Eagle (Sp & W)
	Rough-legged Hawk (W)
	American-golden Plover (Sp & F)

	American Avocet (Sp & F)
	Baird's Sandpiper (Sp & F)
	Buff-breasted Sandpiper (F)
	Wilson's Phalarope (Sp & F)
	Short-eared Owl (Sp, F, W)
	LeConte's Sparrow (F)
Unlikely to find it here (but this is your best bet)	
	Common Redpoll (F & W)

Big Lake is a state owned property located in northeastern Brown County. One can only bird Big Lake if the gate is open on the west side of the property, (39.970282, -90.547611).

The bluffs near the entrance can be good for winter songbirds. Eastern Bluebirds, Hermit Thrushes, and Cedar Waxwings can be seen here. Continue down the gravel road past the gate until you reach the T. Take a left and go north.

After dog-legging east, there will be a vast grasslands around Big Lake. In the winter, many Bald Eagles and Northern Harriers are seen, and sometimes a Golden Eagle or a Short-eared Owl can be seen as well. Also, in some winters, good sized flocks of goldfinches can be seen here. Siskins and some Common Redpolls have been seen here in winter as well.

Continuing along the entrance road, Big Lake will be to the south and some small ponds are to the north. In recent years, Big Lake has stayed roughly the same water level due to a clogging of the pipe to the river. In wet years, however, when the river is high, Big Lake does flood easily.

Thousands of waterfowl (and sometimes some swans) are seen here. During dry years, shorebirds can be seen here in good numbers. American Avocet, both Godwits, Red Knots, Ruff, and Buff-breasted Sandpipers are uncommon shorebirds that have reported here in numbers.

Before leaving the area, during years when the river is very high, check the agricultural fields west of Big Lake. These fields flood and can be a hotspot for shorebirds.

Chautauqua NWR

Ease of access: Easy, for the most part, depending on how much you have to walk
Duration: Half to full day in the fall, a few hours other times of year
Dominant habitat: Lake, mudflat, and forest

Should find it here	
	All 3 swans (F, W, Sp)
	Greater Scaup (W)
	American-white Pelican (Sp & F)
	Bald Eagle (All)
	American-golden Plover (Sp & F)
	Sanderling (F)
	Baird's Sandpiper (Sp & F)
	Stilt Sandpiper (Sp & F)
	Both dowitchers (Sp & F)
	Wilson's and Red-necked Phalaropes (F)
	Franklin's Gull (Sp & F)
	Common Tern (F)
	Peregrine Falcon (All)
Might find it here	
	Any scoter (F & Sp)
	Snowy Egret (F)
	Little-blue Heron (F)
	Osprey (Sp, Su, F)
	Red-shouldered Hawk (All)
	Sora (Sp & F)
	Black-necked Stilt (Sp & Su)

	American Avocet (F)
	Both godwits (F)
	Ruddy Turnstone (F)
	Buff-breasted Sandpiper (F)
	Lesser-black backed Gull (Sp, F, W)
Unlikely to find it here (but this is your best bet)	
	Piping Plover (F)
	Red Knot (F)
	Sharp-tailed Sandpiper (F)
	Ruff (F)
	Red Phalarope (F)
	Sabine's Gull (F)
	Any Jaeger (F)

Chautauqua is a National Wildlife Refuge property located in Northwestern Mason County along the Illinois River northeast of Havana. This property is widely thought to be the "Shorebird" Capital of Illinois. On a fall day, one could see 15, 20, or if you're lucky, 25 species of shorebirds. The property is productive year-round, but late summer and fall is the best time to bird at Chautauqua. Start your journey at the Eagle Bluffs parking area, (40.376805, -89.977397). To get here turn north onto County Road 1950 off of Manito Road, just south of Buzzville. Between the entrance to the property and the parking lot is a good area to see flocks of passerine birds. Uncommon migrant warblers, like Blackpoll and Mourning Warblers, can be seen. At the Eagle Bluff parking area, one can view both North and South Pools of the refuge.

From here, thousands of birds can be seen during migration. Sometimes they can be close; sometimes not so much, but either way, Chautauqua never disappoints. First, scan from the Eagle Bluff parking area to find the birds. Depending where they are, you can plan your stops around Chautauqua. Typically, to start out, park your car and walk the crossdike northwest. Sometimes only 1 pool is drawn down, but in recent years both pools have been drawn. By November, water is let back into both pools, providing habitat for tens of thousands of waterfowl. Also during November and the early spring months, grebes and loons are reliably seen.

You can walk along the crossdike and anywhere else until October 15th. After that date pay close attention to signage, as parts of the refuge are closed to allow birds to rest. Although uncommon shorebirds can be seen throughout the refuge, the spits just east of the crossdike can be one of the best areas on the property. Usually large gull roosts can take place here and large numbers of uncommon shorebirds like Avocets, plovers, Sanderlings, Ruddy Turnstones, and Phalaropes can be seen. Piping Plover, Curlew Sandpiper, Sharp-tailed Sandpiper, and multiple Ruff have been seen here. Sometimes flocks of passerines can be seen along the crossdike. Many sparrows and finches, including flocks of siskins, can be seen along here. Lark, Nelson's, and Le Conte's Sparrows are uncommon sparrows that can be found here as well. Also look on tops of the dead trees in the northwest part of the south pool as raptors can be found sitting on top of the trees. Golden Eagles and Peregrine Falcons are some of the raptors that can be seen.

After visiting Eagle Bluff, work your way back to the refuge headquarters. Continue back out on Buzzville Road and after going past the village of Buzzville, you'll see the large Chautauqua Headquarters sign just south of Buzzville. Turn on the Headquarters Road and head west until you reach the headquarters parking lot (40.364089, -89.998074).

During migration, anywhere around the headquarters can be loaded with migrating passerines, especially warblers. Many uncommon warbler species like Golden-winged and Cape May can be seen often. Continue on the loop trail that heads north of the parking area. There are three observation decks that look over the south pool along this trail. The middle deck is the best deck for spotting, although all three can be good. Thousands of birds can be seen from the decks. Also, if you have some time and the south pool is low, walk the gravel road, which heads southwest from the headquarters.

Walk along this road and you will reach an area where the

"South end" of the south pool is visible. This is another place where thousands of shorebirds can be seen. Along the road is another area to see large migrant flocks in spring.

Continue back north along Buzzville Road, passing the town and the Eagle Bluff. The road will pass a farm house and will enter a small forest. The road will dogleg right and you'll see a small parking area on the north side of the road, (40.385094, -89.961058). Park here and walk on the trail north, which leads to the lake's edge. This spot is the best on the refuge to see phalaropes, more particularly Red Phalaropes, which are rare, but 2-3 are seen annually. During the first week of September is the best time to see Red-necked Phalaropes, as this time is their peak. Annually, double digit numbers of Red-necked Phalaropes can be seen, with a high count of 40 in 2011. Large flocks of shorebirds like to feed in this area, including large flocks of peeps and Stilt Sandpipers.

Continuing north on Buzzville Road (before reaching the west end of Goofy Ridge), just east of this parking lot. Before reaching the west end of Goofy Ridge, look for a barbed wire fence on the west side of the road along the woods. Next to one of the posts along this fence, you should see at least one (if not many) beer cans, around (40.389227, -89.957139). Stop here and park along the road. This area is called the "Beer Can Spot". Walk to the post, find the small trail that continues into the woods, and walk down the trail down to the water's edge. This is the best place on the refuge to see all five species of peeps. A hundred or more Baird's Sandpipers can be seen here throughout the month of September. Look at the flats between the shore and the dike to the north. This area is the best place to see plovers, Upland Sandpipers, and Buff-breasted Sandpipers. Also large duck, pelican, and gull flocks can be seen here.

Continue on Buzzville Road through Goofy Ridge and turn north onto Main Street, (40.392574, -89.941032). Continue on Main street until it reaches the Goofy Ridge parking area, (40.399479, -89.941882). In and around the parking area, particularly the fall months, watch for large passerine flocks in the forest and shrubs. This is the best place to see migrant Black-throated Blue Warblers during September in Western Illinois. Large warbler flocks can be seen, along with large sparrow flocks (especially Eurasian-tree Sparrows). The flocks can be found between the dip and the control gates (the water control structure). Also, watch for Ospreys and Green Herons just north of the dike along the slough just to the north.

Continue on past the control gates. There sometimes can be a very strong dead fish smell (and throughout Chautauqua in general). Start looking for the mudflats, typically the best time to visit here is July through early September, as usually by mid-September, the water has receded and the flats are a considerable distance away. When there is a small amount of grass growing on the drier flats, look for plovers, more particularly, Buff-breasted Sandpipers, as this is arguably the best spot in the state to see Buff-breasted Sandpipers under the right conditions. The flats just north of the dike, on the south end of Clear Lake, are also a good area to see these along with other shorebirds. If it's not a hot day and you have time, walk the 1.5+ miles down the dike to where it curves, sometimes the shorebirds like to congregate in this corner of the North Pool. Also look for "beach shorebirds" whenever the sand spits are just showing up, just southeast of the curve. These shorebirds would consist of Sanderlings, Ruddy Turnstones, and Red Knots. Also look for terns, particularly Least Tern as a few juveniles have been seen here during the fall months.

Columbia Bottom State Conservation Area

Ease of access: Easy
Duration: 2-3 hours (spring might require more time)
Dominant Habitat: Forest, Agriculture, and Marsh

Should find it here	
	All 3 swans (Sp, F, W)
	Greater Scaup (Sp, F, W)

Northern Shoveler (F, W, Sp)

Green-Wing Teal (F, W, Sp)

Blue-Winged Teal (F & S)

Northern Pintail (F &W)

All 3 mergansers (F&W)

Northern Bobwhite (All)

American-white Pelican (All)

Both bitterns (Sp, Su, F)

Black-crowned Night Heron (Su &
  F)

Bald Eagle (All)

Red-tailed Hawk (All)

Red –shouldered Hawk (Sp &F)

Northern Harrier (All)

Peregrine Falcon (All)

Common Gallinule (Sp, Su, F)

Peeps (small shorebird species) (Sp
  & F)

Stilt Sandpiper (Sp & F)

Franklin's Gull (Sp & F)

Herring Gull (All)

Ring-Billed Gull (All)

Willow Flycatcher (Sp & Su)

Sedge Wren (Sp, Su, F)

Marsh Wren (Sp

American Pipit (Sp & F)

Yellow-breasted Chat (Sp,F)

Blue Grosbeak (Sp, Su, F)

Bobolink (Sp & F)

Orchard Oriole (Sp, Su, F)

Warblers* (see notes below)

Yellow-billed Cuckoo (Sp &Su)

American Tree Sparrow (W)

Eurasian-tree Sparrow (All)

Might find it here
Snowy Egret (Sp, Su, F)
Little-blue Heron (Su & F)
Osprey (Sp, Su, F)
American Avocet (F)
Both Godwits (Sp & F)
Sanderling (F)
Baird's Sandpiper (Sp & F)
Buff-breasted Sandpiper (F)
Red-necked Phalarope (Sp & F)
Laughing Gull (Su & F)
Lapland Longspur (Sp & W)
Snow Bunting (F & W)
Grasshopper Sparrow (Su & F)
Le Conte's Sparrow (F)
Rusty Blackbird (Sp, F, W)
Brewer's Blackbird (Sp, F, W)
Short Eared Owl (F, W, & Sp)

Unlikely to find it here (but this is your best bet)
Scoter sp (Sp & F)
Tricolored Heron (Sp, Su)
Glossy Ibis (Sp & Su)
Prairie Falcon (W)
Golden Eagle (F, W)
Sabine's Gull (F)
Chestnut-sided Longspur (Sp, F,W)
Alder Flycatcher (Sp)
Harris's Sparrow (Sp, F, W)
Yellow-headed Blackbird (Sp, Su, F)

This 4,318-acre area is one of the best kept birding secrets in the Midwest. It is an 'urban oasis', the likes of which are few and far between. The area includes a view of the confluence of the Missouri and Mississippi rivers, more than 6.5 miles of river frontage, about 800 acres of bottomland forest, and a 110-acre island.

The Missouri Department of Conservation manages Columbia Bottom to create diverse habitats that include shallow wetlands, bottomland hardwoods, prairie, and cropland. Of course, these habitats provide great cover for migrating birds, but there are a surprising number of species that have nested on the property as well.

To get here, follow Columbia Bottom Road to the large "Blue Gooses" entrance sign. Turn here and take an immediate left into towards the Nature Center (which is closed on Monday and Tuesday). The Nature Center itself is informative, but here you can get a map and talk to one of the naturalists, who are generally up-to-date on any sightings of significance. From the Nature Center there are many routes one could take to explore the park, and their productivity really depends on the season, water levels, and vegetation present at any given time. It is recommended to get some suggestions from the naturalists as far as possible routes or budget extra time to find the birds, because one thing is certain…the birds are there! The one habitat that is reliably fantastic, especially during spring migration, is the bottomland forest! Warblers in the forest during spring and fall migration can be simply astounding. Hard-to-get species, such as the Connecticut and Cerulean Warblers, are more common here than in the surrounding region. Much of the forest habitat is to the east, which is not a bad thing, because to get to it one will pass through open agriculture fields, prairie, shrub habitat, wetlands, and backwater sloughs, that are all part of the migration flyway. Columbia Bottom has a three trails that are equally productive (though not necessarily at the same time) and two board walks that allow easy access to slough and wetland habitat. Depending on the season and conditions, mosquitos can be a bit annoying, so plan accordingly. Also, Columbia Bottom floods with more regularity than some of its surrounding wetlands, so check its status before you make the trip.

Copperhead Hollow

Ease of access: Generally easy, depending on the weather conditions on the road and the number of hunters
Duration: 2-3 hours
Dominant habitat: Forest

Should find it here	
	Wild Turkey (All)
	American Woodcock (Sp, Su, F)
	Whip-poor Will (Sp, Su, F)
	Red-headed Woodpecker (All)
	Yellow-bellied Sapsucker (Sp, F, W)
	Pileated Woodpecker (All)
	White-eyed Vireo (Sp, Su, F)
	Wood Thrush (Sp, Su, F)
	Ovenbird (Sp, Su, F)
	Louisiana Waterthrush (Sp & Su)
	Yellow-throated Warbler (Sp & Su)
	Northern Parula (Sp, Su, F)
	Worm-eating Warbler (Sp & Su)
	Yellow Warbler (Sp & Su)
	Kentucky Warbler (Sp & Su)
	Hooded Warbler (Sp & Su)
	Yellow-breasted Chat (Sp & Su)
	Summer Tanager (Sp, Su, F)
	Scarlet Tanager (Sp, Su, F)
	Lincoln's Sparrow (Sp & F)
	Fox Sparrow (Sp, F, W)
	Blue Grosbeak(Sp, Su, F)
	Orchard Oriole (Sp, Su, F)
	Eurasian-tree Sparrow (All)

Might find it here	
	Broad-winged Hawk. (Sp, Su, F)
	Red-shouldered Hawk (All)
	Acadian Flycatcher (Sp & Su)
	Willow Flycatcher (Sp & Su)
	Bell's Vireo (Sp & Su)
	Winter Wren (Sp, F, W)
	Blue-winged Warbler (Sp & Su)
	Prairie Warbler (Sp & Su)
	Purple Finch (Sp, F, W)
Unlikely to find it here (but this is your best bet)	
	Cerulean Warbler (Sp & Su)

Copperhead Hollow is a state owned property in western Jersey County. First and foremost, it should be noted that this property is heavily hunted in the fall and winter, so be very careful. That said, this property is a little gem and is "under-birded." Despite its small size, one can see more birds at Copperhead Hollow than at nearby Pere Marquette State Park.

Located a couple miles southwest of Fieldon, Copperhead Hollow could be considered as being in the middle of nowhere. Exit off of Nutwood Road onto Belt Road (39.097867, -90.511615). Usually, the northern end of the preserve is not very birdy. However, in the winter months, Hermit Thrushes, Eastern Bluebirds, and Yellow-rumped Warblers can be seen here. After about half a mile, there will be a huge gulch (39.088604, -90.512034). Barred Owls, Red-headed Woodpeckers, Ovenbirds, and Worm-eating Warblers can be seen in these areas. Between this point and where the road opens up, migrant warblers, tanagers and Rose-breasted Grosbeaks are common. Blackpoll Warblers have been seen here before as well.

Stop where the road opens up (at the high point), just before the steep down-hill (39.080293, -90.513343). This spot is a good place to see Hooded and Kentucky Warblers.

Continue down the hill to a riparian/bottomland forest. Right after the drop down the hill, look for breeding species such as Northern Bobwhites, Willow Flycatchers, Bell's Vireos, Prairie Warblers, Blue-winged Warblers, Blue Grosbeaks, and Orchard Orioles.

Continue down to the parking lot (39.076345, -90.514416). During the winter months huge flocks of sparrows can be seen, including wintering Field and Fox Sparrows. The creekbed area east of the parking lot is a good area to see Louisiana Waterthrushes, Yellow-throated Warblers, and if you're lucky, even a Cerulean Warbler.

Turn around and go back towards the entrance. Continue west along Nutwood Road. From here to the town of Nutwood, one could see many Louisiana Waterthrushes, Yellow-throated Warblers, and Northern Parulas, especially during the spring months. Wood Ducks and Red-shouldered Hawks can be seen along here as well. In the winter months, one could find Belted Kingfisher, all the woodpeckers, Red-breasted Nuthatch, Winter Wren, Kinglets, Fox Sparrows, Purple Finches, and Eurasian Tree Sparrows.

Double T

Ease of access: Easy
Duration: 1 hour
Dominant habitat: Wetland and prairie

Should find it here	
	Mute Swan (All)
	Ring-necked Pheasant (All)
	Willow's Flycatcher (Sp & Su)
	Marsh Wren (Sp, Su, F)
	Yellow Warbler (Sp, Su, F)
	Blue Grosbeak (Sp, Su, F)
	Bobolink (Sp & F)

Might find it here	
	Northern Bobwhite (All)
	Green Heron (Sp & Su)
	Rough-legged Hawk (W)
	Long-billed Dowitcher (Sp)
	Short-eared Owl (W)
	Bell's Vireo (Sp & Su)
	Sedge Wren (Sp, Su, F)
	Yellow-breasted Chat (Sp & Su)
	Rusty Blackbird (Sp, F, & W)
	Orchard Oriole (Sp, Su, F)
Unlikely to find it here (but this is your best bet)	
	Upland Sandpiper (Su)

Double T is a state owned property in central Fulton County, about 9 miles northwest of Canton, Illinois. The prairies and old mining lakes create a diverse habitat that attract a nice mix of breeders and migrants.

Start from Canton and head north on Highway 78 then turn west onto Cypress Road. You will reach the intersection with County Highway 21 (40.589759, -90.035990). Continue west, but after passing this intersection, you have reached the east edge of Double T.

There will be ponds on both sides of the road. During migration, thousands of waterfowl, Mute Swans, and shorebirds can be seen on these ponds and other lakes throughout the property. Also, during the summer, the marshy areas around here can be good areas for Common Gallinules and Marsh Wrens.

Continue on Cypress Road, pass the boat ramp and the large slough on the north side. Past the slough there will be prairie habitat on both sides of the road (40.596928,-90.106193). This is a great area in the spring and summer to hear some specialty breeding birds, like Upland Sandpiper and Bobolinks. Also, listen for Ring-necked Pheasants and Willow Flycatchers. Sometimes the area on the north side will be flooded, which provides foraging habitat for shorebirds.

East St. Louis Area

Ease of access: Generally easy
Duration: Half a day
Dominant habitat: Lake, wetland, and urban

Should find it here	
	Snowy Egret (Sp, Su, F)
	Little-blue Heron (Su & F)
	Western Kingbird (Sp & Su)
	Eurasian-tree Sparrow (All)
Might find it here	
	Mississippi Kite (Sp & Su)
	Yellow-crowned Night Heron (Sp, Su, F)
	Surf Scoter (W & Sp)
Unlikely to find it here (but this is your best bet)	
	Black-bellied Whistling Duck (Su)
	Neotropic Cormorant (Sp, Su, F)
	Brown Pelican (Su)
	White Ibis (Su & F)
	Painted Bunting (Sp & Su)

East St. Louis is overlooked and under-appreciated as a birding hotspot. From southern waders to western riparian breeding birds, this area is worth a visit for those wanting to see some local rarities.

Horseshoe Lake State Park

Horseshoe Lake is a State Park located in southwestern Madison

County, in Granite City. Start at the entrance off of Highway 111, at (38.699567, -90.065635). Continue west and follow the road as it doglegs south. Sometimes some ducks and waders can be seen along the lake shore here.

Eventually you will come to the causeway after the road doglegs back west. The area south of the road can be filled with thousands of ducks and coots during winter and spring. Most years, this area is drained during mid-summer. July and August is the best time to check this particular hotspot. Dozens of Little Blue Herons and Snowy Egrets can be seen, and it is not uncommon to spot both species of Night-Heron as well. Other rarities, like White Ibis, have been reported here. Also watch for some shorebirds as hundreds can be seen foraging here.

Turn around and continue back on the road to the entrance, but instead of going back to the highway, continue on north. There are many pull offs to view the lake. Loons and Horned Grebes are seen often, as well has an occasional Scoter, Long-tailed Duck, or winter gulls. An adult Long-tailed Jaeger was reported here in the summer of 2016. Eventually you will reach an area where the road goes past water on both sides of the road, (38.707706, -90.073681). This area is another good place to see Little Blue Herons, Snowy Egrets, and some marsh birds, like Soras. You will eventually come to two fish ponds on the north side of the road. This is the best chance to see Eurasian-tree Sparrows. There are some other places to view the lake along here as well, which is the best area to see some winter gulls.

Continue back to the entrance (the junction with Highway 111), the fields to the east of here can flood during some years. Many shorebirds and gulls can be seen here, such as Marbled Godwit and Franklin's Gulls. This spot has produced some amazing birds as well, including a Mountain Bluebird in 2011. Also watch for the mudflats on Canteen Lake, on the west side of Highway 111, south of the Horseshoe Lake SP entrance, south of the railroad tracks. This is sometimes a good place to see hundreds of shorebirds, including Ruff. Also check the Borrow Pits during winter months. This is a hotspot for winter gulls, such as Glaucous and Greater Black-backed

Gulls. This area is along Mueller Lane, just east of the Gateway Raceways.

Cahokia Mounds

Another productive area is Cahokia Mounds State Park, located only a few minutes south of Horseshoe Lake State Park. From the entrance of Horseshoe Lake, take Highway 111 south, past Interstate 70/55. The area just west of Highway 111 and south of the Interstate, is an amazing area in the summer to see Snowy Egrets and Little Blue Herons, (38.661777, -90.093721). Once you reach the dead end with Collinsville Road, take Collinsville Road east, then take a left (south) on Ramey Street (38.658540, -90.058712), and you have entered into Cahokia Mounds State Park.

The first place to look for birds are the ponds just to the east of the main parking area. The best time to check these is during July and August, when multiple adult and immature Yellow-crowned Night Herons can be seen. This is one of the only places in the state to see them frequently. Also check for more Snowy and Little Blue Herons, overhead a Mississippi Kite flying over, or Cattle Egrets in the lawn. Also check the wet areas just south of the main parking area for more breeding birds including Purple Martins.

Front Street

Finally, take a trip down to Front Street during the summer months. Be careful around here since this is busy area and people are not used to birdwatchers in the area. First, stop at the substation just north of the casino (38.628743, -90.174165), along Riverpark Drive, just east of Front Street. Here, many Western Kingbirds can be seen. In 2017, five pairs were seen here. They have also been seen up and down Front Street as well. Turn north onto Front Street and continue on.

After about two miles, the road splits. Take the road that doglegs east and park right after you pass a small gated building (38.640213, -90.171661).This is the only place to see Painted

Buntings regularly in Illinois. This is also a good area to see Little-blue Herons, Mississippi Kites, Bell's Vireos and Orchard Orioles.

Emiquon National Wildlife Refuge

Ease of access: Easy
Duration: Half a day, depending on the time of year
Dominant habitat: Lake, marsh, and prairie

Should find it here	
	All 3 swans (Sp, F, W (Mute is All year round)
	Greater Scaup (Sp, F, W)
	Northern Bobwhite (All)
	Common Loon (Sp, F)
	American-white Pelican (All)
	Both bitterns (Sp, Su, F)
	Black-crowned Night Heron (Su & F)
	Bald Eagle (All)
	Rough-legged Hawk (W)
	Virginia Rail (Sp, Su, F)
	Common Gallinule (Sp, Su, F)
	Black-necked Stilt (Sp, Su, F)
	Dunlin (Sp & F)
	Stilt Sandpiper (Sp & F)
	Long-billed Dowitcher (Sp &F)
	Franklin's Gull (Sp & F)
	Black Tern (Sp, Su, F)
	Willow Flycatcher (Sp & Su)
	Bell's Vireo (Sp & Su)
	Sedge Wren (Sp, Su, F)
	Marsh Wren (All?)
	American Pipit (Sp & F)

Yellow-breasted Chat (Sp, Su, F)

Blue Grosbeak (Sp, Su, F)

Bobolink (Sp & F)

Orchard Oriole (Sp, Su, F)

Eurasian-tree Sparrow (All)

Might find it here	

Long-tailed Duck (F & W)

Red-throated Loon (Sp & F)

Eared Grebe (Sp & F)

Red-necked Grebe (Sp & F)

Snowy Egret (Sp, Su, F)

Little-blue Heron (Su & F)

White-faced Ibis (Sp, Su, F)

Osprey (Sp, Su, F)

American Avocet (F)

Both Godwits (Sp & F)

Sanderling (F)

Baird's Sandpiper (Sp & F)

Buff-breasted Sandpiper (F)

Red-necked Phalarope (Sp & F)

Laughing Gull (Su & F)

Lapland Longspur (Sp & W)

Smith's Longspur (Sp)

Snow Bunting (F & W)

Prothonotary Warbler (Sp & Su)

Henslow's Sparrow (Su & F)

Grasshopper Sparrow (Su & F)

Le Conte's Sparrow (F)

Nelson's Sparrow (F)

Rusty Blackbird (Sp, F, W)

| **Unlikely to find it here** | |
(but this is your best bet)	

Mottled Duck (Sp)

Surf Scoter (Sp & F)

Pacific Loon (F)

Western Grebe (F)

Western Grebe (F)

Neotropic Cormorant (Sp, Su, F)

Glossy Ibis (Sp & Su)

Sandhill Crane (Sp & F)

Sabine's Gull (F)

Least Tern (Su)

Arctic Tern (Su)

Parasitic Jaeger (F)

Harris's Sparrow (Sp, F, W)

Yellow-headed Blackbird (Sp, Su, F)

Located in Eastern Fulton County, Emiquon is one of the best birding hotspots in Illinois. Its reputation as a premier birding hotspot has grown consistently over the past decade, and rightfully so. This large property will never disappoint.

Start your epic journey at Emiquon from the Intersection of Highways 78/97, and 136. The intersection coordinates are (40.296731, -90.084640).

Before turning north on Highway 78 and going towards the Emiquon area, if its a wet year, go west on Highway 136 for a few miles until you reach Curless Road. Turn right (north) on Curless Road. If the area is flooded, it can hold hundreds of shorebirds and ducks. Also, during the winter months, swans can sometimes be seen in these fields.

Continue back to the intersection of Highway 78/97 and 136. Take Highways 78 and 97 north from here. You will pass a gravel road on the left immediately after passing over the Spoon River. This road leads to an area called the Wilder Track. In recent years it has not been very productive, but in the past it has been excellent for shorebirds. Nowadays, it is a good area to see Short-eared Owls in the winter and Prothonotary Warblers in the summer.

Continue north on Highway 78/97. After a short drive, Thompson Lake will be on your right. The levee and the 3 pull offs before Dickson Mound Road (County Road 9) can be amazing for birding. The south levee is good for Little Blue Herons and Snowy Egrets. The next pull-off, which overlooks the south marshes of Thompson Lake, can be a great area for marsh breeding species. Nesting specialties like Hooded Mergansers, both bitterns, Black-crowned Night Herons, Virginia Rails, Common Gallinules, and Marsh Wrens can be heard and seen often during the spring and summer months. Also, look for both White-faced and Glossy Ibis during May or June. The next pull off, just north of the small S curve in the highway, is a good place to view the south end of the lake and the spit far out to the northeast, upon which hundreds of birds tend to roost. Red-necked Grebe and Little Gull have been seen from this look out. On the spit, many species of ducks, Neotropic Cormorant, Laughing Gull, Least and Arctic Terns, and a even Snowy Owl have been seen. Piping Plover, Whimbrel, Ruddy Turnstones, and Sanderlings have also been reported here. The last pull-off is the best out of the three. The last pull off before you reach the intersection with Dickson Mound Road, is straight across from the spit and the Pump House, which is why it is called the "Pump House Road Pull-off". This is the best place to view the south end of Thompson Lake. This area is the best place to find Neotropic Cormorants in Illinois as they are seen sporadically each year, and are likely nesting somewhere on the lake. All three scoters and Long-tailed Ducks are seen during some years. Red-throated Loons and the 3 rare grebes (Eared, Red-necked, and Western) are usually seen during the fall. Nearly every September, a Sabine's Gull is found here and Laughing Gulls are seen every year here, as well.

The next stop is the "Observatory Area." To get here, exit east off of Highway 78/State Route 97 just north of Dickson Mound Road (County Road 9). This is another area to look for rare big lake birds. Continue north on the gravel road. Check the mudflats south of the boardwalk area when the lake is low, as sometimes hundreds of shorebirds can be seen here. The area north of the boardwalk used to be a marsh and when it was, Mute Swans, both Bitterns, King and Virginia Rails, Soras, Common Gallinules, Black-necked Stilts, and Marsh Wrens regularly nested here. The road eventually makes a turn to the east for a short distance to the north of this area. The grassland area north of this section of the road can be a great area to see Le Conte's and Nelson's Sparrows, and Bobolinks during September and October. The foxtail areas here are the best areas. Rails and other marsh birds are seen as well. This area seems like a good area for Yellow Rail, but it has not been reported here as of yet. The area along the lake here is a great place for waders. Cattle Egrets, Tricolored Heron, and White-faced and Glossy Ibis have been seen here before.

You'll eventually reach the observatory parking lot (40.356914, -90.081743), which is just northwest of the Observation Tower. Park your car here and walk south and go up the Observation Tower. From this area, you can see the middle and northern part of Thompson Lake. This is the best place to see rarities on Thompson Lake. All 3 scoters, Long-tailed Duck, Pacific and Red-throated Loons, all 3 rare grebes, Neotropic Cormorant, both ibis, hundreds of shorebirds, Laughing, Little, Sabine's, California, and Lesser-black backed Gulls have been seen here. Also, on a spring day with very little heat waves, look for Yellow-headed Blackbirds flying around or on cattails straight across from the tower. Continue south along the trail. Between here and the end of the trail, this area is a good place to see Snow Buntings during November and December. Also, the end of the trail is another good area to see LeConte's and Nelson's Sparrows.

Once back in your car, continue back to the highway. Turn back south and turn west onto Dickson Mounds Road (County Road 9). Right after crossing the creek, you'll see a large impoundment on each side of the road. These two places are called the North and South Globe Tracks. Water levels frequently change here so it is not great all the time, but usually it is amazing birding here. One can just bird along the road or park at the South Globe parking area (40.341738, -90.092922 and walk to find birds. Thousands of shorebirds can be seen during the right periods. Great birds like Neotropic Cormorant, Anhinga, both ibis, Snowy Plover, Piping Plover, Red Knot, Sharp-tailed Sandpiper, multiple Ruffs, Arctic and Royal Terns have been recorded here. During winter months, Rough-legged Hawks are seen frequently here.

Continue along Dickson Mounds Road. The road doglegs to the

north. Prairie Road is the first left you can take. Take Prairie Road east. This road will take you back to Highway 78/State Route 97, but not before you pass through some excellent habitat. Between here and until you reach the highway again, you'll see grassland field after grassfield field. Late summer is the best time to check this area. Willow Flycatchers, Bell's Vireos, Sedge Wrens, Henslow's and Grasshopper Sparrows, Blue Grosbeaks, and Bobolinks can be heard and seen throughout this area. Also, during spring, check for Smith's Longspurs flocks.

Continue to Highway 78/97 and continue north. Turn northeast onto Clack Road. This road is a good place for spring migrants, wintering sparrows, and summering Willow Flycatchers, Bell's Vireos, and Yellow-breasted Chats. One year, both Connecticut and Black-throated Blue Warblers were seen here. Continue north to Highway 24 and turn right (east). You'll see a large cattle farm just north of the highway. During November, hundreds if not a thousand or more of Brewer's Blackbirds can be seen here.

Jim Edgar Panther Creek State Fish & Wild Area

Ease of access: Generally easy, sometimes a lot of hunters
Duration: 1-3 hours
Dominant habitat: Prairie and forest

Should find it here	
	Ring-necked Pheasant (All)
	Rough-legged Hawk (W)
	American Woodcock (Sp, Su, F)
	American Pipit (Sp & F)
	Yellow Warbler (Sp & Su)
	Bobolink (Sp & F)

Might find it here	
	Northern Bobwhite (All)
	Wild Turkey (All)
	Green Heron (Sp, Su, F)
	Short-eared Owl (Sp, W)
	Whip-poor-will (Sp, Su, F)
	Lapland Longspur (Sp, W)
	Lark Sparrow (Sp & Su)
	Grasshopper Sparrow (Sp & Su)
	Henslow's Sparrow (Sp, Su, F)
	Western Meadowlark (All?)
	Eurasian-tree Sparrow (All)
Unlikely to find it here (but this is your best bet)	
	Northern Shrike (Sp & W)

Jim Edgar State Fish & Wildlife Area is a large state owned property in northern Cass County. Jim Edgar has a diverse set of habitats, which largely consist of grasslands and forests. There are, however, a few lakes and some marsh areas.

Start from the small town of Chandlerville, along the Sangamon River in northern Cass County. Take Creek Road southeast out of the town. Creek Rd will T with Reed Road in 3.5 miles. This stretch is actually not a bad place to bird watch. Lots of woodland birds can be seen along here. Birds like Eastern-screech Owl, Pileated Woodpecker, Hermit Thrush, Yellow-rumped Warbler, Fox Sparrow, and Purple Finch can be seen or heard during most winters. Also American Woodcocks, Barred Owls, and Whip-poor-wills can be heard during spring nights along this road. Wood Ducks and Hooded Mergansers are sometimes seen at the pond northeast of the T intersection (40.024691, -90.111178).

Turn right onto Reed road (the name will change back to Creek Road) and continue south. After traveling on the road for 2-3 miles, the road makes a 'curvy dogleg" and continue straight east. For about the next half mile, this is a good place to see a Northern Shrike during winter months. It has been seen of both sides of the road.

Turn south onto Cox Rd. (County Rd. 11). The area along the road, just south of the intersection, is a vast area of prairies. Ring-necked Pheasants can be seen regularly. Also, Short-eared Owls in the winter, Western Meadowlarks in the spring, and Northern Bobwhites, Sedge Wrens and Henslow's Sparrows in the summer can be heard or seen here. Cox Rd. doglegs to the west. In the winter check the power lines and surrounding shrubs as this is the best place on the property to see Northern Shrikes. It seems they prey upon the American and Eurasian-tree Sparrows in the shrubs here. This is also a good area to see Rough-legged Hawks during the winter.

Turn south onto Watkins Road. Between here and the T intersection with Gridley Road, look for Northern Shrikes or Western Meadowlarks if you have yet to see one yet. Turn west onto Gridley Road, and not far after turn left (south), into the Gridley Lake parking lot. Some ducks can be seen here in the winter, Wilson's Snipes along the shoreline in the spring, and Green Herons and Spotted Sandpipers in the summer. Also, you can walk the trail that goes around the lake. Breeding birds, such as Summer Tanagers, Rose-breasted and Blue Grosbeaks, can be seen here regularly.

Meredosia Area

Ease of access: Generally easy based on water levels
Duration: Half a day
Dominant habitat: Lake, forest, and prairie

Should find it here	
	American-white Pelican (Sp, Su, F)
	Bald Eagle (All)
	Black-necked Stilt (Sp)
	Semipalmated Sandpiper (Sp & F)

Short-eared Owl (Sp, F, W)

Red-breasted Nuthatch (Sp, F, W)

Northern Mockingbird (All)

Prothonotary Warbler (Sp & Su)

Grasshopper Sparrow (Sp & Su)

Lark Sparrow (Sp & Su)

Blue Grosbeak (Sp, Su, F)

Orchard Oriole (Sp, Su, F)

Eurasian-tree Sparrow (All)

Might find it here

Surf Scoter (Sp & F)

Ring-necked Pheasant (All)

Least Bittern (Su)

Black-crowned Night Heron (Sp, Su, F)

American Avocet (Sp & F)

Hudsonian Godwit (Sp & F)

Red Knot (F)

Sanderling (Sp & F)

Baird's Sandpiper (Sp & F)

Buff-breasted Sandpiper (F)

American Woodcock (Sp, Su, F)

Red-necked Phalarope (Sp & F)

Franklin's Gull (Sp & F)

Iceland Gull (W)

Western Kingbird (Sp & Su)

Winter Wren (Sp, F, W)

Pine Warbler (Sp & F)

Vesper Sparrow (Sp & F)

Henslow's Sparrow (Sp & Su)

Pine Siskin (Sp, F, W)

Unlikely to find it here (but this is your best bet)

Black Scoter (F)

Yellow-crowned Night-Heron (F)

Swainson's Hawk (Sp)

The diverse habitats that make up the Meredosia area help create a region that hosts a diverse set of birds. This area encompasses habitats like forests, grasslands, marshes, a river, and lakes. One could spend a whole day birding this area.

First start birding up in the bluffs that are directly east of Meredosia. Starting along Deepe Road, which you can access by turning east off of Highway 67 (39.825646 , -90.507764). Deepe Road is a good road for birding, especially during migration. Thrushes and warblers can be seen in good numbers in some years. Also, huge numbers of Red-breasted Nuthatches can be seen. During one fall, 35 were seen during one late September morning. The best spot for these and other passerines is (39.832716,-90.49358), where a shrubby forest is on one side of the road and a pine forest is along the other side of the road. Uncommon birds like Olive-sided Flycatcher, Red-breasted Nuthatches, Veerys, Golden-winged, Mourning, Cape-may, Wilson's, and Canada Warbler, Red Crossbills, and Purple Finches have been seen here in the past. This location is the only spot in Morgan County where Pine Warblers have summered and, in 2017, a pair of Pine Warblers likely nested.

Also, the Meredosia Hill Prairie, a Illinois Audubon property, is worth a stop in the fall and winter. Turn southeast onto Trones Road off of Arenzville Road. The brush along here is a good area to see many sparrows during the fall. In the winter, Hermit Thrushes, Yellow-rumped Warblers, Fox Sparrows, and Purple Finches can be regularly seen here. House Wren, Orange-crowned Warbler, and Field Sparrows have been seen during the winter here as well. Also, on a fall day with northwest winds, take time to hawkwatch from the hill prairie west of the road. Park your car at (39.855451, -90.461630), and walk up the hill prairie to the open bluff. During some days, hundreds of hawks can be seen migrating overhead.

Next, continue on Arenzville Road towards Meredosia. During a wet year, which happens every few years, check for small flooded fields between Deepe Road and Highway 67. Shorebirds have used these fields in the past. Also, a Swainson's Hawk was seen here in the spring of 2017.

In wet years, the flooded fields along Highway 67, north of Arenzville Road can be spectacular. The best fields, by far, are the flooded fields north of the creek and west of Highway 67, about a half mile north of the Arenzville Road intersection. There is a dirt road that heads west of Highway 67 north of the creek, (39.851086, -90.505489). This road is the best place to view these fields. The best field is the field north of the dirt road, but both can be great. Hundreds of shorebirds use these fields in May, and many uncommon shorebirds have been seen here in the past. American Avocets, Willets, both Godwits, Ruddy Turnstones, Sanderlings, and Western Sandpipers have been seen here before. Also Franklin's Gulls and nesting Black-necked Stilts have been seen here as well.

Continue back to Arenzville Road and turn west onto Koch's Lane, (39.840196, -90.505489). The grassland along here to the north is a good place to see Ring-necked Pheasants. Just west of the grassland area are agricultural fields that flood regularly. There are four fields, which is how this little hotspot got the name, "Four Corners." To be clear, this spot is only good when it is flooded, but when it is, it can be very good indeed! Birds like Cinnamon Teal, Eared Grebe, White-faced Ibis, Swainson's Hawk, Whimbrels, Least Terns, Yellow-headed Blackbirds, and Great-tailed Grackle have been seen in the past here. Also, nesting birds during wet years include Hooded Mergansers, Least Bitterns, Virginia Rails, and Common Gallinules. The prairie area just north of Four Corners is a good spot for Western Meadowlarks in the spring and Sedge Wrens and Henslow's Sparrows in the summer. If you come here during August, check the ditch for Yellow-crowned Night Herons.

Continue west on Koch's Lane, until you reach Beach Road. This area is good for Blue Grosbeaks and Grasshoppers Sparrows in the summer. Turn north onto Beach Road, and before going down to the lake, go by the headquarters area and park in the trail parking lot (39.845170, -90.558216). Walk the trail down to the slough and back. The pines here are good for Red-breasted Nuthatch, Kinglets, Fox Sparrows, and Siskins. The parking lot area is good place to see

Lark Sparrow in the summer.

Continue along Beach Road on down to Meredosia Lake. The area between the drop-down and the opening area to the south end of the lake can be good for migrant warblers during the spring and fall. Also, this is a good area to see Prothonotary Warblers in the summer and Winter Wrens during the winter.

To view the south end of Meredosia Lake, park along the road at (39.857329,-90.557052). Here the trees open up and you can see the whole south end of the lake. During dry months, when the river is low, this area encompasses mudflats and sand spits were thousands of shorebirds can be seen. Birds like American Avocets, Godwits, Willets, Red Knots, Sanderlings, Buff-breasted Sandpipers, and Red Phalarope have been seen here before. Also in the fall, despite the hunting, hundreds of ducks and gulls congregate in this area. All three Scoters, Laughing Gull, California Gull, and both the Lesser and Great Black-backed Gull have also been seen from here. The forests between here and the boat ramp can be full of migrants during migration months. During the winter months, many Bald Eagles can be seen here. At the boat ramp (39.870454, -90.549652) hundreds of ducks can be seen to the north. Long-tailed Duck, Eared Grebe, and many Common Loons have been seen from this location.

Just after the road doglegs back to the east, the slough area can be full of birds. Some great birds have been reported here, including Spotted Towhee, Harris's Sparrows, Common Redpolls, and more.

Continue east along County Line Road and after passing over a ditch, look at the large grassland north of County Line Road. During the winter months, look for Western Meadowlark's and Short-eared Owls. In summer months, Henslow's Sparrows can be heard. Ring-necked Pheasants are frequently seen in this area as well. Other oddities, such as Snowy Owl and a Sandhill Crane have been found in this area as well.

Continue along County Line Road, turn onto Highway 67, and then turn west onto Honey Point Road. Continue west on the road past the village and park along the road right before you reach the levee, (39.890942, -90.525297) . The prairie north of here is a great place to hear several Western Meadowlark's during the spring.

This is another good spot to see a Short-eared Owl. Walk on up to the levee. From here one can usually see hundreds of ducks and during dry years, migrating shorebirds stop here as well. Also, many Bald Eagles and occasionally a Northern Shrike can winter along the levee.

Before leaving the area, if you're here during the summer, check out the areas south of Meredosia. Western Kingbirds have nested here in recent years. The best place to see the birds is at the two electrical substations, (39.819881,-90.562856), (39.789681, -90.561140). The fence along Old Naples Road, just west of the railroad tracks south of Meredosia, is the best place to see adults with juvenile kingbirds in July (39.815320, -90.562014). Other common birds seen in these areas include Northern Mockingbirds, Grasshopper Sparrows, Blue Grosbeaks, Orchard Orioles, and Eurasian-tree Sparrows. The fields east of Smith Lake, northeast of Naples are worth a check from migrating waterbirds as well.

Peoria Lake

Ease of Access: Usually easy, depending on traffic
Duration: 2-3 hours
Dominant habitat: Lake

Should find it here	
	Red-breasted Merganser (Sp, F, W)
	American-white Pelican (Sp & F)
	Common Loon (Sp & F)
	Peregrine Falcon (All)
Might find it here	
	Greater Scaup (W & Sp)
	White-winged Scoter (W)
	Long-tailed Duck (W)
	Red-throated Loon (F & Sp)

	Sanderling (F)
	Baird's Sandpiper (F)
	Franklin's Gull (Sp, F)
	Iceland Gull (W)
	Lesser black-backed Gull (Sp, F, W)
	Glaucous Gull (W)
	Common Tern (Sp, F)
Unlikely to find it here (but this is your best bet)	
	Brant (F)
	Surf Scoter (Sp, F, W)
	Black Scoter (F)
	Eared Grebe (Sp & F)
	Red-necked Grebe (Sp & F)
	California Gull (All)
	Greater-black backed Gull (W)

Peoria Lake is actually part of the Illinois River. The city of Peoria sits upon the western shore of the lake, which makes the lake more accessible than other reservoirs discussed in this book. This lake has a good reputation, being a hot spot for good ducks, loons, grebes, and gulls. The best times to visit this area are late October-early April, but some shorebirds can be seen from the south end during fall migration if the river is very low.

Start this adventure from RiverPlex (40.693820, -89.580916). Park your car and walk out towards the south end of the lake. During very cold winters, when most of the lake is iced up, huge numbers of gulls can be seen here due to the moving barge traffic that keeps the water mostly open. If the river is low, look at the mudflat area directly to the east for roosting pelicans, shorebirds, gulls, and terns. During fall and winter months, watch for large diving ducks, such as Scoters, feeding in the southern part of the lake.

Continue on back east on Interstate 74, and exit onto Highway 150/24 north. Watch for Peregrine Falcons along the bridge hunting the Rock Pigeons. Continue along the highway until you have reached the Eastport Marina area, and turn west to go down towards the Marina. The best times to visit are during late fall and early winter. Large flocks of gulls can be seen on the outer walls of the marina, allowing more chances to see winter gulls, including California Gulls. Watch for large flocks of diving ducks, scoters, and Long-Tailed ducks in this area as well. Also, look for unusual grebes and loons from here as many Eared Grebes and Red-necked Grebes have been seen as well.

Pere Marquette State Park

Ease of access: Generally easy, some hikes moderate to difficult
Duration: 2-4 hours
Dominant habitat: Forest

Should find it here	
	Wild Turkey (All)
	Bald Eagle (All)
	Broad-winged Hawk (Sp, Su, F)
	Whip-poor Will (Sp, Su, F)
	Ruby-throated Hummingbird (Sp, Su, F)
	Red-headed Woodpecker (All)
	Pileated Woodpecker (All)
	White-eyed Vireo (Sp, Su, F)
	Fish Crow (Sp, Su, F)
	Wood Thrush (Sp, Su, F)
	Ovenbird (Sp, Su, F)
	Worm-eating Warbler (Sp & Su)
	Prothonotary Warbler (Sp & Su)
	Kentucky Warbler (Sp & Su)
	Hooded Warbler (Sp & Su)
	Northern Parula (Sp, Su, F)

	Pine Warbler (All?)
	Yellow-throated Warbler (Sp & Su)
	Summer Tanager (Sp, Su, F)
	Scarlet Tanager (Sp, Su, F)
Might find it here	
	Ross's Goose (Sp, F, W)
	Northern Bobwhite (All)
	Red-shouldered Hawk (All)
	Lesser-black backed Gull (W)
	Acadian Flycatcher (Sp & Su)
	Blue-headed Vireo (Sp & F)
	Philadelphia Vireo (Sp & F)
	Red-breasted Nuthatch (Sp, F, W)
	Winter Wren (Sp, F, W)
	Swainson's Thrush (Sp & F)
	Blackburnian Warbler (Sp & F)
	Black-and-white Warbler (Sp & F)
	American Redstart (Sp, Su, F)
	Cape-may Warbler (Sp & F)
	Wilson's Warbler (Sp & F)
	Canada Warbler (Sp & F)
	Blue Grosbeak (Sp, Su, F)
	Purple Finch (Sp, F, W)
	Pine Siskin (Sp, F, W)
Unlikely to find it here (but this is your best bet)	
	Cerulean Warbler (Sp & Su)

Pere Marquette State Park is a large preserved forest habitat in southwestern Jersey County where visitors come for the views from the lookouts along bluffs and the Bald Eagles during the winter. Pere Marquette is where some of the first warblers arrive in central Illinois for nesting during March and April.

Start from the headquarters, which is just east of Highway 100,

(38.973124, -90.542927). Across the street from here you'll see the small marina and the Illinois river. During the winter, the parking lots and roads are full as many people come to the park to watch eagles, as this area is a huge wintering territory for this species. If it is a cold winter, look for gulls and Bald Eagles along the river. In some years, huge flocks of gulls form here. Lesser Black-backed Gulls, Iceland Gulls, and even California Gulls have been seen here. Also, along the river, and in Lower Stump Lake (best seen from a small parking lot north of the marina (38.973675, -90.547433) can hold hundreds of ducks in the spring and fall. Also, in the early fall, Lower Stump Lake sometimes can hold several hundred shorebirds, including Western and Baird's Sandpipers. This area is the best area to see and hear Fish Crows in the Illinois River area. It is not uncommon to see more than 20 Crows here in an afternoon.

Continue back to the Visitor Center and take the Scenic Drive that heads northeast from here and into the forest. The area around the Visitor Center can be "birdy" at times, especially in the winter months, when Yellow-rumped Warblers, Hermit Thrushes, both Kinglets, and Purple Finches can be seen. Besides the scenic lookouts that allow spectacular views of the confluence region, the areas between the visitor's center and Army Road is the best area in spring and early summer to hear, or even see, a Worm-eating Warbler, as a few pairs seem to like the huge draws along here. Also Summer and Scarlet Tanagers, Wood Thrushes, Eastern-wood Pewees and Eastern Screech Owls are some of many birds that use this area as their breeding territory.

Before continuing along Scenic Drive, turn right to Army Road. Army Road is the best place in Central Illinois for Hooded Warblers. Although they are seen throughout the park, this is the best area for them. Also Acadian Flycatchers and Kentucky Warblers are commonly seen in this area.

Continue back to Scenic Drive northeast to Mailbox Road and turn here. Mailbox Road is a great place for Pine Warblers in the spring and Red-breasted Nuthatches in the winter. Also Yellow-bellied Sapsuckers sometimes frequent this area. The best location for the Pine Warblers is (38.997642, -90.497480).

Continue along Mailbox Road to Graham Hollow Road, where you will turn sharply to the right (south). After zig-zagging through a gulch, it will lead you to the creekbed/forest area. Keep going to the intersection of Graham Hollow Road and Army Road (38.985686, -90.492421). Besides the Hooded Warblers, this area hosts many breeding warblers, including Louisiana Waterthrush, Northern Parula, Yellow-throated Warbler, American Redstart, and some years a breeding Black-and-White Warbler or even a Cerulean Warbler. This area also hosts a few pairs of White-eyed Vireos. Keeps your eyes to the sky as Broad-winged Hawks or maybe even a Red-shouldered Hawk might pass by.

Before leaving the area, if its the fall, Gilbert Lake might be worth a peek. From Graham Hollow Road, take Highway 100 West, past the Brussles Ferry. Take the first gravel road that goes south off the highway west of the Ferry. Park in the parking lot (38.967770, -90.498365), and walk the gravel road that heads south. Near the parking lot, look for Green Herons, Red-headed Woodpeckers, and possibly even a Prothonotary Warbler. After a short hike (~0.5 miles), you will come upon the lake. If it is at the right water level, hundreds of teal and pelicans, thousands of shorebirds and some gulls will be using the flats. Black-necked Stilts, Red Knot, Western Sandpiper, Buff-breasted Sandpiper, and Wilson's Phalarope have been seen here. Look around as Peregrine Falcons and Merlins might be hunting the birds here as well.

Riverlands, Big Muddy NWR (Cora Island Unit), Ted and Pat Jones State Park

Ease of access: Easy
Duration: Half a day, depending on the time of year
Dominant Habitat: River, wetland, and mudflat

Should find it here
All 3 swans (Sp, F, W (Mute is All year round)
Greater Scaup (Sp, F, W)
Northern Shoveler (F, W, Sp)
Green-Wing Teal (F, W, Sp)
Blue-Winged Teal (F & S)
Northern Pintail (F &W)
All 3 mergansers (F&W)
Northern Bobwhite (All)
Common Loon (Sp, F)
American-white Pelican (All)
Both bitterns (Sp, Su, F)
Black-crowned Night Heron (Su & F)
Bald Eagle (All, but huge numbers in W)
Rough-legged Hawk (W)
Northern Harrier (All)
Common Gallinule (Sp, Su, F)
Black-necked Stilt (Sp, Su, F)
Peeps (small shorebird species) (Sp & F)
Stilt Sandpiper (Sp & F)
Long-billed Dowitcher (Sp &F)
Franklin's Gull (Sp & F)
Herring Gull (All)
Ring-Billed Gull (All)
Least Tern (Su)
Black Tern (Sp, Su, F)
Willow Flycatcher (Sp & Su)
Bell's Vireo (Sp & Su)
Sedge Wren (Sp, Su, F)
Marsh Wren (All?)
American Pipit (Sp & F)

	Yellow-breasted Chat (Sp,F)
	Blue Grosbeak (Sp, Su, F)
	Bobolink (Sp & F)
	Orchard Oriole (Sp, Su, F)
	American Tree Sparrow (W)
	Eurasian-tree Sparrow (All)
Might find it here	
	Long-tailed Duck (F & W)
	Red-throated Loon (Sp & F)
	Eared Grebe (Sp & F)
	Red-necked Grebe (Sp & F)
	Snowy Egret (Sp, Su, F)
	Little-blue Heron (Su & F)
	White-faced Ibis (Sp, Su, F)
	Osprey (Sp, Su, F)
	American Avocet (F)
	Both Godwits (Sp & F)
	Sanderling (F)
	Baird's Sandpiper (Sp & F)
	Buff-breasted Sandpiper (F)
	Red-necked Phalarope (Sp & F)
	Laughing Gull (Su & F)
	Lapland Longspur (Sp & W)
	Smith's Longspur (Sp)
	Snow Bunting (F & W)
	Prothonotary Warbler (Sp & Su)
	Warblers* (See notes below)
	Grasshopper Sparrow (Su & F)
	Le Conte's Sparrow (F)
	Nelson's Sparrow (F)
	Rusty Blackbird (Sp, F, W)
	Short Eared Owl (F, W, &Sp)
Unlikely to find it here (but this is your best bet)	
	Scoter sp (Sp & F)

Pacific Loon (F)

Western Grebe (F)

Neotropic Cormorant (Sp, Su, F)

Glossy Ibis (Sp & Su)

Sandhill Crane (Sp & F)

Prairie Falcon (W)

Sabine's Gull (F)

Arctic Tern (Su)

Parasitic Jaeger (F)

Harris's Sparrow (Sp, F, W)

Riverlands (and nearby properties) can be one of the best "peri-urban birding" locations in the United States. Included in this property description are four distinct parcels: Riverlands (Inclusive of Ellis Island and Lincoln Shields), Ted and Pat Jones State Park, and Big Muddy NWR- Cora Island Unit. What makes this area special is not just the fact that it is the confluence two of the biggest rivers in the world, but also that it has so many habitats that are ideal for migratory and nesting birds.

We like to call this area the "Silk Road" of birding. You may not see everything here, but everything can be seen here. When birds get lost or get blown off course, they seem to make their way to the Mississippi or Missouri Rivers…and eventually find their way to Riverlands.

A good spring day can produce well over 100 species. And while that is exciting, the winter months are often when this area turns up its real specialties. Water levels here are managed by the Army Corps of Engineers and can fluctuate significantly, thus impacting the birds one can see along the river. Even when the water is high, however, the region is still a "top spot" for any person who wants to see the birds of the Midwest mixed in with a few rarities.

Riverlands is on the west side of the Mississippi River, directly across from Alton Illinois in what is technically West Alton. If one were to come from the Illinois side of the river (east) across the Alton Bridge on US Highway 67, they should take the first left on to "Riverlands Way" (approaching from the west, take the last right hand turn before the Alton Bridge). Your birdwatching adventure should start immediately!

Elis Island and Lincoln Shields

Turning left (east) back towards the river on an outer road will take you towards Elis Island. The Alton Slough will be to the south. This area can be quite productive from September through May. The water depth here is quite variable and will impact the types of birds that are present, but there will almost always be something to see.

Driving along the slew a parking lot will appear on the right for Ellis Island. During the spring this island can be highly productive for migrating warblers and other song birds. In the winter the trails on Elis Island will give you access to the backwater of the slough... and, very likely, great looks at waterfowl. On the east side of Elis Island Is the main channel of the Mississippi River. It is not uncommon in the winter to have a ducks out on the main channel in front of Elis Island. Long-tailed ducks, Redheads, Goldeneye, Scoters and others are often reported. After a hike you can hop back in the car and continue along the outer road. This will lead you to Lincoln Shields Recreation Area. This area of shallow water on the west side of the Mississippi River is good for waterfowl and gulls. Experienced birders know that one mustn't be complacent when looking at gulls! While there will be a disproportionate number of Ring-billed Gulls and Herring Gulls there are almost always some surprises hanging around Lincoln Shields.

Alton Slough, Rivers' Edge

Heading back toward Riverlands Way, there is a gas station at the corner. It is not a bad idea to stop and check out the body of water directly behind the gas station. Particularly the northeast side, which is not really visible from anywhere else. This body of water is called Teal Pond. In the summer it is very common to see Least Terns hunting for fish here and along the Mississippi River (they nest on the pond on 'nesting barges'). Teal pond "punches above its weight" in terms of species production. Besides ducks and waterfowl it also produces a surprising number of raptors and shorebirds.

Heading south along Riverlands Way, Alton Slough is to the east and various grassland, marsh, and flood plain habitats are to the west. The road here has extra wide shoulders…almost as if it was built for birders! Stop frequently, as there is often something to see, even if you don't see it right away! If the water is low, particularly in spring and late summer/early autumn, the shorebirds here can be quite numerous. In the winter the ducks, gulls, and eagles are plentiful.

It is always a good idea to stop by the Audubon Center at Riverlands. They always have the latest information on what has been seen, where things are being seen, and how recently they have been seen.

Driving along the river is very likely to produce good species. Don't ignore the incredible habitat to the west, however, where sparrows, swans, snipes, pipits, and Short-eared Owls can be seen. Riverlands Way makes a hard right into Ted and Pat Jones State Park (which is discussed in the next section). Keep going straight until the road takes a hard left, back towards the river. This road takes you to the Lock and Dam. Spring and fall are good months for this hotspot, but winter is when this little stop can really shine. On one particularly cold, dank winter afternoon we observed 7 species of gulls here…in 20 minutes. And while this spot does not always produce great birds, it is literally 30 seconds out of the way, so it is certainly not a problem to check it out.

Ted and Pat Jones State Park

Immediately past some maintenance buildings on the west side of the road, Riverlands Way takes a turn into "Ted and Pat Jones State Park", sometimes referred to as "Jones Confluence Park". This drive wanders through mixed agricultural land. Don't let the flat topography and seemingly homogeneous vegetation fool you. This area is good for a number of species. Often times after a rain there will be large puddles. Stop at every one of them and check out the edges for shorebirds and sparrows. There are many types sparrows that can be found here and in the winter it is particularly good for longspurs. After 4 miles you will come to the actual state park. To be completely honest, it is not much to look at. Sure, it is neat to see the two great rivers come together, but in reality if the birding wasn't good, we probably wouldn't venture down here all that often. That said, birdwatching here can be quite good, but is a bit "hit or miss". A small forest parcel directly at the confluence can hold a number of passerines during migration, but it is just as likely to produce very little. It is reliable for Orchard Oriole, American Kestrel, and a few species of sparrows, but is otherwise highly inconsistent. That said, when it is "on", it is really good. It is always worth a stop, but maybe not worth a lot of time.

Big Muddy NWR -Cora Island Unit

Driving back towards Hwy 67 on Riverlands Way take a left (west) onto Wise Road(~200 meters past the Audubon center). Since you are there, you might as well take a quick look at Teal Pond from the opposite corner. Driving southwest on Wise Road you will come to an intersection. Take a left onto Red School Road. After a little less than a mile, turn left onto Orton Road. This road will dead end at the Heron Pond Avian Observatory. This is a particularly good spot to see overwintering waterfowl such as the Trumpeter Swan. It is also a great place to see many sparrows species, particularly in winter. It is probably one of the least utilized, yet most productive, birding spots in the entire Riverlands complex.

Returning to Red School Road continue to head southeast until the intersection of Cora Island Road. There is a small cemetery on the south side of the road that serves as a landmark. Cora Island Road almost always has some standing water in the spring and fall. Because of this it is very reliable for shorebirds and wading birds. Drive slowly so as to not scare birds, as they are often very close to the road. This road terminates at Big Muddy National Wildlife Refuge, Cora Island unit. Park in the parking lot and walk around for a bit. If you visit during the spring you can rightfully expect to see several species of sparrows/grosbeaks. Summer tanagers and thrushes can be found in the (relatively sparse) wooded areas. While there are a number of species that could easily be spotted here, sparrows are what takes the cake. Even if the birding is not great (which it normally is), it is great place to walk and get a feel for the unique habitats of the area.

Sand Ridge State Forest

Ease of access: Easy, just watch out for the car loads of hunters during late fall
Duration: A few hours
Dominant habitat: Forest

Should find it here	
	Wild Turkey (All)
	American Woodcock (Sp, F)
	Whip-poor Will (Sp, Su, F)
	Red-breasted Nuthatch (All?)
	Pine Warbler (All?)
	Purple Finch (Sp, F, W)
Might find it here	
	Black-billed Cuckoo (Sp, Su, F)
	Northern-Saw Whet Owl (Sp, F, W)
	Olive-sided Flycatcher (Sp & F)
	Yellow-bellied Flycatcher (Sp & F)
	Veery (Sp & F)
	Blackburnian Warbler (Sp & F)
	Cape-may Warbler (Sp & F)
	Mourning Warbler (Sp & F)
	Canada Warbler (Sp & F)
	Blue Grosbeak (Sp, Su, F)

	Red Crossbill (F, W)
	Pine Siskin (All?)
Unlikely to find it here (but this is your best bet)	
	Northern Goshawk (W)
	Townsend's Solitaire (F & W)
	Connecticut Warbler (Sp)
	Black-throated Blue Warbler (Sp, F)
	Pine Grosbeak (W)
	White-winged Crossbill (F & W)
	Common Redpoll (W)

Sand Ridge State Forest is located in northwestern Mason County, a few miles west of the small town of Manito. This large mostly coniferous forest offers a unique pine habitat that is actually rare in Central Illinois. First things first: this property is heavily hunted in the fall, so use extreme caution if birding here October through January.

The first option to come into the state forest is from the west side. Head east out from the village of Goofy Ridge along 2300 E. Eventually, this road will make a long dogleg to the north, and a smaller paved road will continue east, and still have the same name (2300N); continue along this road. After about a quarter of a mile, there will be the numerous dying Virginia and Jack Pines along the road. Pull off along the road, (40.392496, -89.918129). During crossbill invasion years, large flocks of Red Crossbills can be seen and heard. A few White-winged Crossbills can be seen within the flocks as well. Red-breasted Nuthatches and Pine Siskins can be seen as well. Large warbler flocks can be seen during May and September with many specialties like Cape-may and Mourning seen here.

From this location to the property Headquarters/Pine Campground area is usually good for spring migrants. Just drive with your windows down and listen for large flock of birds calling or flying over the road, stop, and search for birds! Some days it's "birdy" and some days it may seem like there's not a bird to be found (but that is birding, right?). The open areas just west of the headquarters can be a good area for Green Herons, American Woodcocks, and Prairie Warblers during the summer. Some of the largest flocks can be seen along the road north and northeast of the headquarters, (north of Pine Campground) (40.391556, -89.869365). Hundreds of birds including, thrushes, warblers, sparrows, and grosbeaks can congregate here. Although nothing terribly unusual or rare has been found here, it's amazing to see how many birds can be seen in a small area.

Pine Campground is just east of the Headquarters. If one were to camp here during the winter months, one can hear many owls, including possibly a Northern Saw-whet Owls. During the spring months one may hear American Woodcocks and Whip-poor-wills. This is also a good place to see nesting Pine Warblers during the spring months.

Another way to enter the state forest is from the south. Travel on Manito Road until you reach Bishop Road, (40.347987, -89.876989). Continue along Bishop Road north into the park. This road can be truly amazing during spring migration. On one morning in late May, the authors observed 70 species along this road. The "mega-flock" included, 40 thrushes, 200 warblers of 21 species, 30 tanagers, and 40 butnings. It was spectacular. Of course, everyday will not be like this, but there is a chance!

Continue north on 2600 E. from the Pine Campground. From here to the Oak Campground area is a good area to see Olive-sided Flycatchers on top of dead trees during May and September. Also, the Archery area, (just west of this road), is a great area to see many Black-billed Cuckoos.

Once you have reached the Oak Campground sign along the right (east) side of the road, you are officially in "Saw-whet" territory, (40.405818,-89.866015). During the winter months Northern Saw-whet Owls are known to congregate here. Listen at night for this beautiful little owl. Also listen for American Woodcocks and Eastern Screech Owls.

Just north of here, a gravel road heads straight west. Take this road. Along this road, until you reach County Highway 15, can be magical during some winters. Rarities like Northern Goshawks, Townsend's Solitaires, and Pine Grosbeaks have been seen and heard here during recent years. Both crossbills can also been seen sporadically. Pine Warblers nest at the large parking area, and many Hermit Thrushes and Purple Finches can be seen around the pump house buildings.

Check the Jake Wolf Fish Hatchery across the County Highway 15 (40.431064, -89.892937). Park at the large Visitor Center parking area and look at the ponds to the west. Surf Scoters, Snowy Egrets, and Little Gulls are some uncommon birds that have been found.

Sanganois and Surrounding Areas

Ease of access: Moderate, depending on water levels and hunter traffic. One lane road leading all the way back to the "Good birding areas" of this refuge.
Duration: 3-4 hours on the best days, a quick stop on other times
Dominant habitat: Bottomland forest, lake, and agricultural

Should find it here	
	Trumpeter Swan (Sp & W)
	Tundra Swan (Sp & W)
	Wild Turkey (All)
	Ring-necked Pheasant (All)
	American-white Pelican (Sp, Su, F)
	Bald Eagle (All)
	Semipalmated Plover (F)
	Baird's Sandpiper (F)
	Stilt Sandpiper (F)
	Short-billed Dowitcher (F)
	Wilson's Phalarope (F)
	Winter Wren (Sp, F, W)

	American Redstart (Sp, Su, F)
	Lincoln's Sparrow (Sp & F)
	Rusty Blackbird (Sp, F, W)
Might find it here	
	Greater Scaup (Sp & W)
	Snowy Egret (Su & F)
	Little-blue Heron (Su & F)
	Osprey (Sp, Su, F)
	Sora (Sp & F)
	American-golden Plover (F)
	American Avocet (F)
	Sanderling (F)
	Western Sandpiper (F)
	Buff-breasted Sandpiper (F)
	Red-necked Phalarope (F)
	Franklin's Gull (F)
	Short-eared Owl (Sp & W)
	Peregrine Falcon (All)
	Red-breasted Nuthatch (Sp, F, W)
	Northern Mockingbird (All)
	Grasshopper Sparrow (Sp & Su)
	Western Meadowlark (All?)
	Pine Siskin (Sp, F, W)
Unlikely to find it here (but this is your best bet)	
	Black Scoter (W)
	Ruff (F)
	Northern Shrike (W)
	Loggerhead Shrike (All?)

Sanganois is a state owned property located in mostly southwestern Mason County (it is also located in some parts of Cass and Schuyler counties). Although it is heavily hunted during the fall and winter months, the lakes can be great for shorebirds and the outer barren-land landscape can sometimes hold surprises. Under the right conditions, Sanganois can be as productive as any property in Central Illinois.

Start by going north on Highway 78 out of Chandlerville. Continue on the highway on past the entrance sign for Sanganois. Continue north for another 1-2 miles to a large grassland strip on the west side of the road. Turn west on E County Road 300 N, (40.104979, -90.154656). The cattle pasture to the north, is a great place to see Cattle Egrets during the summer and fall months, although in recent years they have not been so reliable. Also, look for Short-eared Owls during winter months and Ring-necked Pheasants year round in the grassland strip to the south of the road. If it is a wet year, check to see if the fields west of the cattle farm are flooded. In spring, American Avocet, both Godwits, and Red-necked Phalaropes can be seen.

As you continue west on E 300 N be sure to check the agricultural fields. In winter, hundreds of swans can be seen. Continuing west, you will come to North County Road 600 E. Turn left (south) on N 600 E. After about a mile, you'll come to an intersection with E County Road 200 N, turn west (right) onto this road, (40.104979, -90.154656). The area northwest of this intersection is a good area to see Northern Mockingbirds and Eurasian Tree Sparrows.

After about approximately three miles of driving west, there will be a gravel road that heads north; turn north here, (40.091651, -90.291878). The shrubs along here can be full of sparrows and other birds. If the road is flooded the gate will be closed. This area (beyond the gate) is really only productive from late-July through late-September. Outside of this period it is advised to continue down the gravel road. Continue along this gravel road for a few miles through many twists and turns, and stop at the Chain Lake parking area/boat ramp. The areas between the gate/headquarters area and the parking lot is a good area to see some bottomland birds, like Winter Wrens during the winter months.

At the parking lot for Chain Lake, (40.123867, -90.309752), there is a crossdike (provided it is not duck hunting season). Park your car in the parking lot and walk along the crossdike. Both sides

84

are often very low and have extensive mudflats. Thousands of shorebirds can be seen here, and (under the best conditions) it's one of the best shorebird spots in Illinois. One may have to walk out on the levee to best see the shorebirds. Some amazing shorebirds have been seen here during some falls. Ruffs and a Sharp-tailed Sandpiper are the best shorebirds that have been seen. Other goodies that are possible are American Avocets, Godwits, Sanderlings, Red Knots, all 5 peeps, Buff-breasted Sandpiper, and Red-necked Phalaropes. Also during the late fall months, many Franklin's Gulls can be seen here and Sabine's Gull is a rare visitor. If there is plant growth and you visit in late September, Soras, Bobolinks and (if you're lucky) Nelson's Sparrow can be seen here as well.

Before leaving the area, walk the dirt road that goes north of the parking area. After about a half mile, the road will dogleg east, and you'll see some tall pines. Sometimes, this area can be full of birds. In good years, many Red-breasted Nuthatches can be seen here. Migrant flycatchers like Olive-sided, Blue-headed and Philadelphia Vireos, and uncommon migrant warblers like Blackburnian, Bay-breasted, and Cape-may can be seen here as well. Also, check the open area east of these forests for Northern Shrikes during winter.

Siloam Springs State Park

Ease of access: Generally Easy
Duration: Half a day
Dominant habitat: Forest and agricultural

Should find it here	
	Wild Turkey (All)
	Broad-winged Hawk (Sp, Su, F)
	Whip-poor-will (Sp, Su, F)
	White-eyed Vireo (Sp, Su, F)
	Wood Thrush (Sp, Su, F)

Ovenbird (Sp, Su, F)

Worm-eating Warbler (Sp & Su)

Louisiana Waterthrush (Sp & Su)

Blue-winged Warbler (Sp & Su)

Northern Parula (Sp, Su, F)

Yellow Warbler (Sp, Su, F)

Yellow-throated Warbler (Sp & Su)

Yellow-breasted Chat (Sp & Su)

Summer Tanager (Sp, Su, F)

Might find it here

Northern Bobwhite (All)

Black-billed Cuckoo (Sp & F)

Chuck-wills-widow (Sp, Su, F)

Acadian Flycatcher (Sp & Su)

Black-and-white Warbler (Sp, Su, F)

Prothonotary Warbler (Sp & Su)

Mourning Warbler (Sp)

Hooded Warbler (Sp & Su)

Prairie Warbler (Sp & Su)

Pine Warbler (All?)

Lark Sparrow (Sp, Su, F)

Henslow's Sparrow (Sp & Su)

Bobolink (Sp & F)

**Unlikely to find it here
(but this is your best bet)**

Bewick's Wren (Sp & Su)

Cerulean Warbler (Sp & Su)

Siloam Springs State Park is a large upland forest habitat located between the Mississippi and Illinois Rivers. It is located only about 35 minutes east of Quincy and 35 minutes west of Meredosia and covers parts of Adams and Brown Counties. One could see a good mix of northern and southern breeding birds in the summer months. In the spring, this is one of the best spots in Central Illinois for migrating songbirds.

Although all times of year can be good for birding here, spring and early summer is the best time to visit Siloam Springs (especially May and June). There are also some great birding areas southeast of the park, which this area is the best place to start. Turn off of Highway 104 north onto 370th Street (39.807434, -90.837075) about 1-2 miles east of Fishhook. Continue along this road as it makes a few bends and turns. After a couple miles, the road changes to 395th Street and heads straight west. It then makes a lengthy dogleg before reaching the Brown County line. This area is good to see Yellow Warblers and Orchard Orioles in Pike County. Continue and you will see a sign for Brown County. This is a good area to see Yellow-breasted Chats. Continue over the creek and the field just east of this road and north of 055 N (39.848994,-90.850936). This is a great place to hear American Woodcocks, Willow Flycatchers, Bell's Vireos, and sometimes, Sedge Wrens and Henslow's Sparrows. The best area to see Henslow's Sparrows is about 1 mile north along 325 E (the road name changes many times again) in some grassy areas just east of the road (39.859586, -90.856022). Also, listen for Barred Owls, Whip-poor-wills, and Blue-winged Warblers.

You will come to the intersection with 175 N near the Buzzville church and cemetery (39.866289, -90.864369). Take this west, as this road will lead you into the east entrance of the state park. After about a half mile, look to the south and you should see a property filled with scrap material (39.866421, -90.871729). For a few years, a pair of Bewick's Wrens summered and possibly nested here. Only birdwatch along the road; don't walk onto the property. From here to the east end of the park, is a great area to see many "scrubby breeders," such as Blue-winged and Prairie Warblers. There are several spots along here that are good little hot spots, but the best location is about a quarter of a mile west of Little Missouri River on either side of the road (39.874392, -90.891834). Also, in May, the grassy field just south of the road before you reach the state park is a great place to see Bobolinks.

After going into the park, you will pass by a huge gulch, (39.875922, -90.907772). This is the best place to see Worm-eating

Warblers in the park. Also, Wood Thrushes and Ovenbirds are common along here. The next place to check out is what we call the "warbler parking lot", which on the map is called "Hunter Lot 1". After passing the gulch, you will pass a big pine forest and a parking lot to the right. Ovenbirds, Pine, and Kentucky Warblers nest around here. In mid-May, check for Connecticut, Mourning, Wilson's, Canada and other migrant warblers as well. It is possible to see a Black-billed Cuckoo, as a few pairs summer in the park. From here until the T intersection with 300 E/State Park Road is a good area to see large migrant flocks of songbirds. There is a small chance that one may see a Prairie warbler in this area, but they aren't that reliable here. Before going south into other areas of Siloam Springs, go to the Equestrian Campground. Take 330 E north from the T intersection and turn east onto N 1000th Ave. This area is a good place to see a pair of Lark Sparrows that summer here. Continue along 1000th ave until you reach the campground on the south side. This campground is a another great place for migrants. Many migrants have been seen here including Blackburnian, Bay-breasted, Golden-winged, and even a Mourning Warbler.

Continue back to the T intersection and continue south. Stop near the headquarters and check the area west of the headquarters, as this is the best place to find nesting Bewicks Wrens (though they have not been reported here since 2015). This area is another good place to see Black-billed Cuckoos and many Summer Tanagers as well.

The next area is our favorite part of the park. Just south of the headquarters, keep and turn left, after awhile, stay straight and don't turn right because that road will lead you down to the lake. The area just after this intersection is another great area for Worm-eating Warblers. The road will eventually take a huge drop into the creek bottom area. Right after the drop, there is a gravel road that goes right from the road, take this. The areas between the intersection and the back park area is the best place in the parking to see Louisiana Waterthrush, Yellow-throated Warbler, Northern Parula, and if you're very lucky, possibly a Cerulean Warbler. Continue back to the dead end parking area (39.884065, -90.921151), as this area is great for birds. Broad-winged Hawks, Black-billed Cuckoos, Northern Waterthrush, and Mourning Warblers have been see from here before. This is the best area in the park to see Black-billed Cuckoos. Also, during the spring of 2017, a pair of Bewick's Wrens were found here as well, but they did not stay at this location.

Continue back to the road, turn left and continue the loop around the creek bottom. You'll likely see the same birds as the previous gravel road, as if you miss them there, you are likely to find them here, as well as a slightly better chance to see a Cerulean Warbler.

Before continuing into the east side of the park, go check out the concession building down by the lake. Food and drinks are sold here. Also, many hummingbird feeders are set up in the spring and summer, where one could see many hummingbirds here. Also Summer Tanagers are common here. In the spring, there's a small chance a Common Loon can be seen on Crabapple Lake.

Go back towards the headquarters and continue east on State Park Road. You will eventually pass a small restoration prairie on your left and a gravel road just to the west of this. Turn on the gravel road and take it down to the lake. Park at the end of the road (39.888181, -90.939562). Walk the small gravel causeway just north of the parking area. This area is a good place to see Green Herons, Belted Kingfishers, and Prothonotary Warblers. Also, in the nearby woods, is the only area in the park that one could find a Hooded Warbler.

Before leaving the area, check out the Buckhorn Unit and County Road 605 E east of the park. To get to Buckhorn Unit, take the east entrance out of the park, at the Buzzville church take a left to the northeast onto 175 N. Continue on this for a few miles until you get to the intersection with 400 N (39.899714, -90.835100). Take this road until it dead ends after about a mile at a grass parking area. Be careful, as the road is not great. Use your best judgment before going here. This is one of only two reliable areas in recent years to hear Chuck-wills-widows in Central Illinois. American Woodcocks, Whip-poor-wills, Barred Owls, and Yellow-breasted Chats can be heard here as well.

Continue back to 450 E and continue back south. Just before

getting to Buzzville, turn east onto 200 N. Take this for several miles. Ridge View Winery is also along here (in case you need some wine for dinner later!). Then take 595 E south down to the small village of Morrelville. Turn left on 065 N then onto 605 E. After the road drops to the creek area, stop your car. This is another great area for breeding birds in the early summer. Acadian Flycatchers, Yellow-throated Vireos, Wood Thrushes, Ovenbirds, Louisiana Waterthrushes, Yellow-throated Warblers, and Northern Parulas can be seen around here. Also, this is your best shot to see Cerulean and Hooded Warblers around this area.

Spring Lake

Ease of access: Easy
Duration: 2-3 hours
Dominant habitat: Lake and wetland

Should find it here	
	Mute Swan (All)
	Bald Eagle (All)
	Marsh Wren (All?)
Might find it here	
	Greater Scaup (W)
	Wilson's Phalarope (Sp)
	Short-eared Owl (W)
	Merlin (Sp & F)
	Willow Flycatcher (Sp & Su)
	Bell's Vireo (Sp & Su)
	Sedge Wren (Sp, Su, F)
	Prothonotary Warbler (Sp, Su)
	Le Conte's Sparrow (F)
	Bobolink (Sp, F)
	Purple Finch (Sp, W)

Unlikely to find it here (but this is your best bet)	
	Sandhill Crane (Sp & F)
	Northern Shrike (W)

Spring Lake State Fish and Wildlife Area is located in southwestern Tazewell County. This area is very heavily hunted for ducks, but is most known for the large numbers of swans (more particularly the Mute Swans).

Start by heading west on County Highway 21 off of Manito Road (the intersection is (40.463638, -89.783197)). You will eventually reach the small village along the east end of Spring Lake, and continue west out onto the causeway , which goes over the middle part of the lake. Many Mute Swans, ducks, and Bald Eagles can be seen. Also, lots of swallows can be seen during fall months. Then turn southwest onto State Park Road which borders the west end of Spring Lake. Watch for more water birds on the lake. Scoters, grebes, and loons can be seen here in some years.

Once you have reached the large boat parking area (40.450198, -89.896096), continue south on the road before heading west into the Spring Lake Bottoms. Also, check for bird flocks in the woods just east of the southeast part of the lake. Large passerine flocks can be seen in the cedar forests. Continue back to the boat ramp parking area. Take the road that heads west to the house/restaurant (40.448751, -89.897826). This road will intersect with 1200 E. Look for Eurasian Tree Sparrows at this intersection, as most times, they are abundant here.

Take 1200 E south and you will see the Spring Lake bottoms on both sides of the road. You can also quickly head north for a mile and see some more bottom-land area along the west side of the road. During wet years, thousands of waterfowl can be seen here, as well as flocks of shorebirds during spring. Many times, decent numbers of breeding-plummaged Wilson's Phalaropes can be seen spinning in the water. The area south of the restaurant, can be one of the best places in Central Illinois to see Northern Shrikes during winter months (40.443977, -89.899955). Also nesting birds like Willow Flycatcher,

Bell's Vireo, and Marsh Wren can be heard here.

Spunky Bottoms and Farmland

Ease of Access: Generally easy depending on water levels
Duration: 2-3 hours
Dominant habitat: Wetland, forest and agricultural

Should find it here	
	Bald Eagle (All)
	Semipalmated Plover (Sp & F)
	Semipalmated Sandpiper (Sp & F)
	Short-billed Dowitcher (Sp & F)
	Prothonotary Warbler (Sp, Su, F)
	Fox Sparrow (Sp, F, W)
	Lincoln's Sparrow (Sp & F)
Might find it here	
	American Wigeon (Sp & F)
	Hooded Merganser (All?)
	Little-blue Heron (Su & F)
	Snowy Egret (Su & F)
	Red-shouldered Hawk (All)
	Rough-legged Hawk (W)
	Black-necked Stilt (Sp & Su)
	Baird's Sandpiper (Sp & F)
	Long-billed Dowitcher (Sp & F)
	Wilson's Phalarope (Sp & F)
	Franklin's Gull (Sp & F)
	Orchard Oriole (Sp, Su, F)
Unlikely to find it here (but this is your best bet)	
	Snowy Owl (W)
	Prairie Falcon (W)

Spunky Bottoms is a Nature Conservancy property along the Illinois River in Brown County. Once a farm land, its now a wetland system. Before reaching Spunky Bottoms, if visiting during the winter, check the agricultural fields south of the creek, and south of Highway 104 in Pike County. Some good birds have been seen here in the past. Snowy Owls, Prairie Falcon, and Smith's Longspurs are a few good finds for this area.

Spunky Bottoms is seasonal. Its productivity as a "hot spot" depends on its water levels. A few years ago, a levee breached and the levee hasn't been fixed. So, the water levels all depend on the river levels. Before this, Spunky Bottoms was a huge wetland, where both bitterns and King Rails nested.

Start on the south side of the property, along La Grange Road, east of 1625 E at the Merwin parking area (39.893574, -90.588015). If there is water here, check for ducks and shorebirds. Birds like Snowy Egrets, Little Blue Herons, Marbled Godwit, Buff-breasted Sandpipers, and hundreds of Franklin's Gulls have been seen here before. Some migrant warblers can be seen here as well.

If you are able, continue on to 500 N. If the river is really high, the road may be flooded. Between here and 500 N, look for more bottom areas to see more waterbirds. The best area is just south of the intersection with 500 N. Willets, Whimbrels, Ruddy Turnstones, and Sanderlings have been seen here before. Take 500 N back, and take the sandy road that goes south. In recent years, this habitat has been damaged by flooding, but this area used to be a great area to see Bell's Vireos and Blue Grosbeaks. Now, it is a good area to see sparrows and good numbers of Eurasian Tree Sparrows.

Continue along La Grange Road north. The next field to the west, again if the river is high, is usually great for waterfowl and shorebirds. When this field flooded one winter, thousands of ducks and geese were seen here. Shorebirds like American Avocet, Willet, Hudsonian Godwit, Ruddy Turnstones, Sanderlings, Buff-breasted Sandpipers, and Red-necked Phalaropes have been seen here before. Also, in the spring of 2017, an Arctic Tern was seen here with many Forster's and Common Terns. Also look for Rough-legged Hawk and Golden Eagle during the winter.

The bluffs between here and the village of La Grange can be very "birdy." In the winter, Eastern Bluebirds, Hermit Thrushes, and Yellow-rumped Warblers can be seen in good numbers. One winter, a Spotted Towhee was seen here.

Before leaving here, check the lock and dam north of here in the winter. This is a good place to see Bald Eagles and sometimes some decent numbers of gulls.

Stump Lake and Surrounding Areas

Ease of access: Moderate, depends on water levels and amount of hunters.
Duration: 2-4 hours
Dominant habitat: Bottomland forest and wetland

Should find it here	
	American Wigeon (Sp, F, W)
	Double-crested Cormorant (All?)
	American-white Pelican (Sp, Su, F)
	Green Heron (Sp, Su, F)
	Bald Eagle (All)
	Red-shouldered Hawk (All)
	Solitary Sandpiper (Sp & Su)
	Least Sandpiper (Sp & Su)
	Red-headed Woodpecker (All)
	Pileated Woodpecker (All)
	Fish Crow (Sp, Su, F)
	Northern Waterthrush (Sp & F)
	Prothonotary Warbler (Sp & Su)
Might find it here	
	Ross's Goose (Sp, F, W)
	Mute Swan (Sp, W)

	Trumpeter Swan (Sp, F, W)
	American-black Duck (Sp, F, W)
	Wild Turkey (All)
	Horned Grebe (Sp & F)
	Snowy Egret (Su & F)
	Little-blue Heron (Su & F)
	Black-crowned Night Heron (Sp, Su, F)
	Osprey (Sp, Su, F)
	Mississippi Kite (Sp, Su, F)
	Semipalmated Plover (Sp & F)
	Long-billed Dowitcher (Sp & F)
	Wilson's Phalarope (Sp & F)
	Winter Wren (Sp, F, W)
	Le Conte's Sparrow (Sp & F)
	Rusty Blackbird (Sp, F, W)
Unlikely to find it here (but this is your best bet)	
	Mottled Duck (F)
	Golden Eagle (Sp & W)
	Great-tailed Grackle (Sp & W)

Stump Lake is a State Fish and Wildlife area in Western Jersey County that contains many habitats. The swampy bottomwood lakes region, to the old, overgrown, dying forest full of large trees and some Cypress Trees along the road to give you the feeling of the South, to the impoundments just off the highway, and the tall bluffs that overlook the property, Stump Lake is a great place to bird in Jersey county. On a good day, if the conditions are right, one can get most of their targets for this area checked off.

Start from the entrance of Stump Lake off of Highway 100 (39.021110, -90.550030). In the winter and spring, look for the flooded impoundments just west of the highway. In some years, these can be loaded with thousands of waterfowl, mostly dabbling ducks like Gadwall and Northern Pintail. That said it pays to be diligent, as recently a Mottled Duck was seen with thousands of ducks. If the water levels are lower here, look for shorebirds here as hundreds of them can be seen in this area.

Continue along Stump Lake Road and you will reach the bottomland forests of Stump Lake. About .5 miles after exiting the highway, the road bends to the southwest. Just before you get to the bend, there are some tall dead oak trees near the road (39.020952,-90.562347). During the summer and early fall, watch for Mississippi Kites either sitting on these trees or flying around. This is the best place to see Mississippi Kites along the Illinois River. Also in this area, Barred Owls, Red-headed and Pileated Woodpeckers can be seen.

Continue west to Upper Sump and Fowler Lake. There are two good parking areas that are also great places to watch for birds (39.020419, -90.564900 and 39.019010, -90.564074). Although this area is heavily hunted during some years, in the spring, there can be some ducks using these waterways. In the late summer, look for waders using the dry lakes. Birds like Snowy Egrets, Little Blue Herons, Ospreys, Mississippi Kites, and Prothonotary Warblers can be seen during the late summer. Rarities like Neotropic Cormorant and Glossy Ibis have been seen here as well. During fall the cypress trees around the south parking lot for Stump Lake (39.019518, -90.563022) can attract good flocks of birds, particularly warblers. Blackburnian, Hooded, and Wilson's Warblers have been seen here before.

Continue back east to the highway. During late winter and early spring, look for raptors soaring over the cliffs during mid-day. These bluffs, particularly the bluff just southeast of the Stump Lake property, is the best place along the Illinois River to see Golden Eagles. A high count of four Golden Eagles were seen on a day in January 2017.

Continue along Highway 100. It is possible to see more ducks and shorebirds in flooded fields west of Highway 100. Drive south for about 2 to 3 miles until you reach Dabbs Road which goes west off of Highway 100 (38.991906, -90.542091).

Before you continue west along Dabbs Road, look for blackbird flocks during the fall and spring months. A Great-tailed Grackle has been reported recently. Also flocks of American Pipits can be seen here during the spring months.

Continue down to the parking lot (38.991539, -90.554193), and walk the small dike the heads west from the parking lot. At times, during spring migration, this area is loaded with passerines in the brush along the dike. Some birds that are possible to see include Winter Wren, Fox Sparrow, and Lincoln's Sparrow. Ducks and more shorebirds can be seen along the dike under right conditions.

Two Rivers - Swan Lake and Pohlman Slough

Ease of access: Moderate, depending on water levels, hunting traffic, and walking long distances
Duration: Up to half a day
Dominant habitat: Lake, forest, agricultural

Should find it here	
	Ring-necked Duck (All?)
	American-white Pelican (Sp, Su, F)
	Bald Eagle (All)
	Least Sandpiper (Sp & F)
	Yellow-billed Cuckoo (Sp & Su)
	Belted Kingfisher (All)
	Red-headed Woodpecker (All)
	Pileated Woodpecker (All)
	Prothonotary Warbler (Sp & Su)
	Yellow Warbler (Sp & Su)
	Eurasian-tree Sparrow (All)
Might find it here	
	Ross's Goose (Sp, F, W)
	Trumpeter Swan (Sp, F, W)

	American Wigeon (Sp, F, W)
	Redhead (Sp, F, W)
	Snowy Egret (Sp, Su, F)
	Little-blue Heron (Su & F)
	Osprey (Sp, Su, F)
	Red-shouldered Hawk (All)
	American-golden Plover (Sp & F)
	Semipalmated Plover (Sp & F)
	Baird's Sandpiper (Sp & F)
	Semipalmated Sandpiper (Sp & F)
	Long-billed Dowitcher (Sp & F)
	Wilson's Phalarope (Sp & F)
	Willow Flycatcher (Sp & Su)
	Bell's Vireo (Sp & Su)
	Fish Crow (Sp, Su, F)
	American Pipit (Sp & F)
	Grasshopper Sparrow (Sp & Su)
	Fox Sparrow (Sp, F, W)
	Rusty Blackbird (Sp, F, W)
Unlikely to find it here (but this is your best bet)	
	Eared Grebe (Sp)
	Western Meadowlark (Sp, F, W)
	Harris's Sparrow (Sp, F, W)

Near the confluence of the Illinois and Mississippi Rivers is a unique blend of habitats that make up Swan Lake and Pohlman Slough. These areas offer an incredible array of birds and interesting natural history. One could spend a whole day birding this area alone.

Swan Lake is a part of Two Rivers National Wildlife Refuge and Pohlman Slough is a part of the Department of Natural Resources in southeastern Calhoun County. The main part of the property is Swan Lake, a large lake that is separated from the Illinois River by a dike. This property also includes some impoundments, forests, and prairies that make this hotspot a host to a diverse set of birds.

The best times to visit are in the spring and fall. Start on the far east side, at the "dike parking area" (38.951152, -90.513836). Turn west off of Illinois River Road onto a gravel road just south of Old Ferry Road. After about 1/2 mile, you will reach the parking lot that connects to the gravel dike that borders Swan Lake. The best birding here will require walking along the dike for up to 1 mile. In the spring you can expect hundreds of duck and geese on the lake. These include Snow Geese, Gadwall, Northern Shoveler, and Ruddy Ducks. Multiple Eared Grebe have been seen during a few springs.

The refuge managers will usually drain the lake in the late summer to grow habitat for ducks in the late fall. In most years, thousands of migrant shorebirds pass through Swan Lake from June to September. Uncommon shorebirds like American Avocet, Marbled and Hudsonian Godwits, Red Knot, Ruddy Turnstone, Buff-breasted Sandpipers, and Red-necked Phalarope have been seen here in recent years. Also, hundreds of waders including Little Blue Herons and Snowy Egrets can be seen during the late summer. A few good gulls have also been seen here including Laughing, Sabine's, Lesser Black-backed, and Iceland Gulls. One recent winter three Harris's Sparrows wintered about ~1/4 miles down the dike. The area around the dike and parking lot is the best place to find Fish Crows in the county.

Next continue along Illinois River Road southwest and after about a mile you will see the Pohlman Slough sign. Travel down this gravel road and turn left at the 'T' intersection. These areas of forests and brush can be quite productive. Flocks of warblers in the fall and flocks of sparrows in the winter often use this area. Continue along the road until you reach the boat launch parking lot (38.942290, -90.504352). The brush around this location usually offers the greatest number of birds. During one recent winter a Brown thrasher and two Harris's Sparrows over-wintered here.

Before turning back onto the Illinois River Road (if you are visiting during winter) look for meadowlarks and blackbird flocks that can be seen on the prairies across the road from the entrance of Pohlman Slough (38.935781, -90.510575) in the winter and spring.

Western Meadowlarks have wintered here and a Yellow-headed Blackbird has been seen here as well.

Continue Southwest along Illinois River road for 1-2 miles until you see the gravel road for Calhoun Wetlands that goes north of the River Road (38.924764, -90.522763). Continue north along this road. In the spring, if the impoundments are flooded, hundreds of ducks and shorebirds will often be seen. If your lucky, American Golden Plovers, Black-necked Stilts, and Wilson's Phalaropes could be seen in April. It also wouldn't be uncommon to spot a Cinnamon Teal. This can also be a good area to see a flock of Savannah Sparrows.

Finally, continue west along the River Road until you reach the sign for the refuge headquarters, around 1/2 mile west of the small village of Deer Plain. Turn north here and you will see the refuge headquarters to the east of the road (38.936189, -90.540395). Look at the bushes in this area as Eurasian Tree Sparrows are often seen here. To the north are more impoundments that may hold hundreds of ducks and shorebirds in the spring. The surrounding fields may have American Golden Plovers and American Pipits. Continue north on the road until you reach the lake parking area, (38.945411, -90.541774). This is another good location to look for waterfowl on the lake. Be on the lookout for swans, as Mute and Trumpeter Swans have been spotted here before. Finally, keep your ears open as Winter Wrens sometimes use this area in the fall.

CHAPTER THREE:
BIRDS

Birding along the Illinois River Flyway is like a box of chocolates, you never know what you are going to get. There are hundreds of species (over 380 to be more specific) that have been recorded here and while there are over 150 breeding species, there are many other species that can show up at just about any time. Given this, we thought it important to give the reader some general idea as to the relative likelihood of spotting particular species and the best places to spot them. Whereas the previous chapter is intended to give you an idea as to what could be expected at particular locations (in terms of habitat and species), this chapter might be useful for planning around 'target species'. For example, if one wanted to see Sabine's Gull, they could reference the table herein and see that it is most likely seen at two locations, Riverlands near Lock and Dam #25 and Emiquon. Further, it is most likely to be spotted in winter. It should be noted that the checklist herein is not exhaustive. There are many species that casually make their way through the region from time to time. We have included only birds that have been recorded reliably from year to year. We should tell you there are a few species (e.g. Roseate Spoonbill, Painted Bunting, and a few others with a rarity of 'five') that are included because we have recorded them a number of times and they are just awesome finds in the region. Also, it warrants mentioning again that the data that has informed our "rarity" and "best places to find this bird" categories, comes from our thousands of hours in the field and other data. Spring and fall migration can be very erratic and the birds are not as reliably found in specific areas during these times.

Ratings

Each species listed in this guide has an individual rating. Honestly, these ratings are actually somewhat arbitrary. However, we mean well. A common complaint we have about most field guides is that they don't indicate the relative abundance of a particular bird in a specific area. There are also some birds (e.g., Dicksissel) that could use some better publication, because the field guides never do them justice in terms of how cool or beautiful they are. We also think that there are some birds (e.g., the Phalaropes) that have really cool behaviors, and if people know about those behaviors, they may hang out a bit longer just to see this bird do its "thing." It is with this in mind that we created our categories.

You will find ratings for '**Wow-Factor**' and '**Rarity**' for each bird. Each of these ratings is based on a 5-point scale. If a bird has fives across the board, this is a dream bird that is really rare, really beautiful, and has some pretty cool behaviors. On the other hand, do not discount those species whose ratings might not be the highest; every bird is special in its own right.

Wow-Factor 🐦🐦🐦🐦🐦 **Rarity** 🐦🐦🐦🐦🐦

Wow-Factor: A "five out of five" in this category would indicate a species of vibrant color or strikingly contrasted plumage. You will definitely have a "bird-gasm" if you see a bird with a five in this category. If you are wondering if you have ever had a bird-gasm, you haven't; if you had one you would know. Also factored in this (extremely scientific) rating is the specie's behavior. For example, the American Woodcock is a crazy looking bird, but what really makes this species stand out is its cool strut and crazy aerial stunt work!

Rarity: A "five out of five" in this category would represent a species that is quite uncommon, not only to this region but in general, such as Cerulean Warbler. This category is a lot less subjective. Scores are based on thousands of hours of observational data collected over many years. It is important to note, however, that some birds that are fairly abundant in the region are actually not very common elsewhere. In other words, some birds could be quite rare globally, but only receive a 2 or 3 because of their relative abundance in this region. Finally, many of the species found in this guide are migratory, so there are times when the birds seem endlessly abundant (e.g. Snow Geese during migration) and times when 'common birds' are noticeably absent. This is why we include the best seasons to see the bird. The 'rarity' rating relates to the relative abundance in the 'best season' to see that particular species.

Lastly, keep in mind the table herein goes across both pages; the name and "Rarity" on the left-hand page and the "Wow-factor," "Best season," and "Hot Spots" on the right-hand page.

Prothonotary Warbler | Riverlands, West Alton, MO

Order: Anseriformes

Family: Anatidae (Ducks, Geese, and Swans)	Rarity
Black-bellied Whistling-Duck (Dendrocygna autumnalis)	🪶🪶🪶🪶
Fulvous Whistling-Duck (Dendrocygna bicolor)	🪶🪶🪶🪶🪶
Snow Goose (Anser caerulescens)	🪶
Ross's Goose (Anser rossii)	🪶🪶
Greater White-fronted Goose (Anser albifrons)	🪶
Brant (Branta bernicla)	🪶🪶🪶🪶🪶
Cackling Goose (Branta hutchinsii)	🪶🪶
Canada Goose (Branta canadensis)	🪶
Mute Swan (Cygnus olor)	🪶
Trumpeter Swan (Cygnus buccinator)	🪶🪶
Tundra Swan (Cygnus columbianus)	🪶🪶

Black-and-White Warbler | Pere Marquette St. Park, Grafton, IL

Wow Factor	Best Season	Hot Spots
🐦🐦🐦🐦🐦	Summer	Spring Lake, Emiquon, East St. Louis
🐦🐦🐦🐦	Summer	Any
🐦🐦🐦	Winter and Spring	Chautauqua and Emiquon
🐦🐦🐦	Spring	Chautauqua and Emiquon
🐦🐦🐦	Winter and Spring	Anywhere along the Illinois River
🐦🐦🐦	Winter	Peoria Lake
🐦🐦	Winter	Emiquon and Meredosia Area
🐦	Any	Any
🐦🐦🐦🐦	Any, Winter usually	Emiquon and Spring Lake
🐦🐦🐦	Winter and Spring	Emiquon and Sanganois
🐦🐦🐦🐦	Winter and Spring	Riverlands

Wood Duck (Aix sponsa)	🪶
Blue-winged Teal (Spatula discors)	🪶
Cinnamon Teal (Spatula cyanoptera)	🪶🪶🪶
Northern Shoveler (Spatula clypeata)	🪶
Gadwall (Mareca strepera)	🪶
Eurasian Wigeon (Mareca penelope)	🪶🪶🪶🪶🪶
American Wigeon (Mareca americana)	🪶🪶
Mallard (Anas platyrhynchos)	🪶
American Black Duck (Anas rubripes)	🪶🪶
Mottled Duck (Anas fulvigula)	🪶🪶🪶🪶
Northern Pintail (Anas acuta)	🪶
Green-winged Teal (Anas crecca)	🪶
Canvasback (Aythya valisineria)	🪶🪶
Redhead (Aythya americana)	🪶🪶
Ring-necked Duck (Aythya collaris)	🪶
Tufted Duck (Aythya fuligula)	🪶🪶🪶🪶🪶
Greater Scaup (Aythya marila)	🪶🪶
Lesser Scaup (Aythya affinis)	🪶
Surf Scoter (Melanitta perspicillata)	🪶🪶🪶
White-winged Scoter (Melanitta fusca)	🪶🪶🪶
Black Scoter (Melanitta americana)	🪶🪶🪶
Long-tailed Duck (Clangula hyemalis)	🪶🪶🪶
Bufflehead (Bucephala albeola)	🪶
Common Goldeneye (Bucephala clangula)	🪶
Barrow's Goldeneye (Bucephala islandica)	🪶🪶🪶🪶🪶
Hooded Merganser (Lophodytes cucullatus)	🪶
Common Merganser (Mergus merganser)	🪶🪶
Red-breasted Merganser (Mergus serrator)	🪶🪶
Ruddy Duck (Oxyura jamaicensis)	🪶

Order: Galliformes

Family: Odontophoridae (New World Quail)	Rarity
Northern Bobwhite (Colinus virginianus)	🪶

Wow Factor	Best Season	Hot Spots
🐦🐦🐦🐦🐦	Summer	Any
🐦🐦🐦	Fall	Chautauqua and Emiquon
🐦🐦🐦🐦	Spring	Meredosia Area
🐦🐦🐦🐦	Fall	Any
🐦🐦	Fall	Any
🐦🐦🐦🐦🐦	Spring	Banner Marsh
🐦🐦🐦🐦	Fall	Chautauqua and Emiquon
🐦🐦🐦	Any	Any
🐦🐦	Winter	Chautauqua and Emiquon
🐦🐦🐦	Fall	Chautuauqua and Stump Lake
🐦🐦🐦🐦	Fall	Any
🐦🐦🐦	Fall	Any
🐦🐦🐦	Fall	Chautauqua and Emiquon
🐦🐦🐦	Fall	Chautauqua and Emiquon
🐦🐦🐦	Fall	Any
🐦🐦🐦	Spring	Spunky Bottoms
🐦🐦	Fall	Emiquon and Peoria Lake
🐦🐦	Fall	Any
🐦🐦🐦	Fall	Emiquon, Peoria Lake, and Meredosia area
🐦🐦🐦	Fall	Peoria Lake, Riverlands
🐦🐦	Fall	Peoria Lake and Meredosia area
🐦🐦🐦🐦🐦	Winter	Peoria Lake, Emiquon, Riverlands
🐦🐦🐦🐦	Winter	Emiquon
🐦🐦🐦🐦🐦	Winter	Peoria Lake
🐦🐦🐦🐦🐦	Winter	Peoria Lake
🐦🐦🐦🐦🐦	Fall	Emiquon
🐦🐦🐦🐦	Winter	Emiquon, Riverlands
🐦🐦🐦	Fall	Emiquon
🐦🐦	Fall	Any

Wow Factor	Best Season	Hot Spots
🐦🐦🐦	Summer	Any

Order: Galliformes *(cntd.)*

Family: Phasianidae (Partridges, Grouse, Turkeys, and Old World Quail)	
Ring-necked Pheasant (Phasianus colchicus)	🐦
Wild Turkey (Meleagris gallopavo)	🐦

Order: Podicipediformes

Family: Podicipedidae (Grebes)	Rarity
Pied-billed Grebe (Podilymbus podiceps)	🐦
Horned Grebe (Podiceps auritus)	🐦🐦
Red-necked Grebe (Podiceps grisegena)	🐦🐦🐦
Eared Grebe (Podiceps nigricollis) (spec)	🐦🐦🐦
Western Grebe (Aechmophorus occidentalis)	🐦🐦🐦🐦

Order: Columbiformes

Family: Columbidae (Pigeons and Doves)	Rarity
Rock Pigeon (Columba livia)	🐦
Eurasian Collared-Dove (Streptopelia decaocto)	🐦
White-winged Dove (Zenaida asiatica)	🐦🐦🐦🐦
Mourning Dove (Zenaida macroura)	🐦

Order: Cuculiformes

Family: Cuculidae (Cuckoos, Roadrunners, and Anis)	Rarity
Yellow-billed Cuckoo (Coccyzus americanus)	🐦
Black-billed Cuckoo (Coccyzus erythropthalmus) (threatened)	🐦🐦🐦

Wow Factor	Best Season	Hot Spots
🐦🐦🐦	Winter	Sanganois, Jim Edger, and Meredosia area
🐦🐦🐦🐦🐦	Any	Sand Ridge, Siloam Sorings, and Copperhead Hallow

Wow Factor	Best Season	Hot Spots
🐦🐦	Fall	Any
🐦🐦🐦	Fall	Peoria Lake and Emiquon
🐦🐦🐦	Fall	Peoria Lake and Emiquon
🐦🐦🐦	Spring and Fall	Peoria Lake, Riverlands, Swan Lake
🐦🐦🐦	Fall	Emiquon

Wow Factor	Best Season	Hot Spots
🐦	Any	Any
🐦🐦	Any	Any
🐦🐦🐦	Spring	Any
🐦	Any	Any

Wow Factor	Best Season	Hot Spots
🐦🐦🐦	Summer	Chautauqua, Columbia Bottom
🐦🐦🐦	Spring	Sand Ridge, Columbia Bottom

Order: Caprimulgiformes

Family: Caprimulgidae (Nightjars)	Rarity
Common Nighthawk (Chordeiles minor)	🐦
Chuck-will's-widow (Antrostomus carolinensis) (threatened)	🐦🐦🐦
Eastern Whip-poor-will (Antrostomus vociferus)	🐦🐦

Order: Apodiformes

Family: Apodidae (Swifts)	Rarity
Chimney Swift (Chaetura pelagica)	🐦

Family: Trochilidae (Hummingbirds)	
Ruby-throated Hummingbird (Archilochus colubris)	🐦
Rufous Hummingbird (Selasphorus rufus)	🐦🐦🐦🐦

Order: Gruiformes

Family: Rallidae (Rails, Gallinules, and Coots)	Rarity
Yellow Rail (Coturnicops noveboracensis)	🐦🐦🐦🐦
Black Rail (Laterallus jamaicensis) (endangered)	🐦🐦🐦🐦
King Rail (Rallus elegans) (endangered)	🐦🐦🐦
Virginia Rail (Rallus limicola)	🐦🐦
Sora (Porzana carolina) (spec)	🐦
Purple Gallinule (Porphyrio martinicus)	🐦🐦🐦🐦🐦
Common Gallinule (Gallinula galeata) (endangered)	🐦🐦
American Coot (Fulica americana)	🐦

Wow Factor	Best Season	Hot Spots
🐦🐦	Summer	Any town
🐦🐦🐦	Spring	Beardstown Area and Siloam Springs
🐦🐦🐦	Spring	Sand Ridge and Siloam Springs

Wow Factor	Best Season	Hot Spots
🐦🐦	Summer	Any
🐦🐦🐦🐦	Fall	Snad Ridge and Siloam Springs
🐦🐦🐦🐦	Fall	Reported only at feeders

Wow Factor	Best Season	Hot Spots
🐦🐦🐦	Fall	Emiquon and Meredosia area
🐦🐦🐦	Summer	Any
🐦🐦🐦	Spring	Beardstown area
🐦🐦	Spring	Emiquon and Beardstown area
🐦🐦	Spring	Emiquon and Beardstown area
🐦🐦🐦🐦🐦	Spring	Any
🐦🐦🐦	Spring	Emiquon and Beardstown area
🐦	Fall	Emiquon, Riverlands

Order: Gruiformes *(cntd.)*

Family: Gruidae (Cranes)	
Sandhill Crane (Antigone canadensis)	🐦🐦🐦
Whooping Crane (Grus americana)	🐦🐦🐦🐦

Order: Charadriiformes

Family: Recurvirostridae (Stilts and Avocets)	Rarity
Black-necked Stilt (Himantopus mexicanus)	🐦🐦
American Avocet (Recurvirostra americana)	🐦🐦🐦
Family: Charadriidae (Lapwings and Plovers)	
Black-bellied Plover (Pluvialis squatarola)	🐦🐦
American Golden-Plover (Pluvialis dominica)	🐦🐦
Snowy Plover (Charadrius nivosus)	🐦🐦🐦🐦
Semipalmated Plover (Charadrius semipalmatus)	🐦🐦
Piping Plover (Charadrius melodus) (endangered, State and Federal)	🐦🐦🐦
Killdeer (Charadrius vociferus)	🐦
Family: Scolopacidae (Sandpipers)	
Upland Sandpiper (Bartramia longicauda)(endangered)	🐦🐦🐦
Whimbrel (Numenius phaeopus)	🐦🐦🐦
Long-billed Curlew (Numenius americanus)	🐦🐦🐦🐦🐦
Hudsonian Godwit (Limosa haemastica)	🐦🐦🐦
Marbled Godwit (Limosa fedoa)	🐦🐦🐦
Ruddy Turnstone (Arenaria interpres)	🐦🐦🐦
Red Knot (Calidris canutus)	🐦🐦🐦
Ruff (Calidris pugnax)	🐦🐦🐦🐦
Sharp-tailed Sandpiper (Calidris acuminata)	🐦🐦🐦🐦

Wow Factor	Best Season	Hot Spots
🐦🐦🐦🐦	Fall	Emiquon and Spunky Bottoms
🐦🐦🐦🐦🐦	Spring	Any

Wow Factor	Best Season	Hot Spots
🐦🐦🐦🐦🐦	Spring	Emiquon, Ted andPat Jones State Park, Meredosia area
🐦🐦🐦🐦🐦	Fall	Chautauqua
🐦🐦🐦	Fall	Chautauqua, Riverlands
🐦🐦🐦	Spring	Chautauqua and Merdosia area
🐦🐦🐦	Spring	Emiquon, Riverlands
🐦🐦	Spring	Chautauqua and Emiquon
🐦🐦🐦	Spring	Chautauqua and Emiquon
🐦🐦	Any	Any
🐦🐦🐦	Fall	Big Lake and Chautauqua
🐦🐦🐦🐦	Spring	Emiquon and Spunky Bottoms
🐦🐦🐦🐦🐦	Spring	Any
🐦🐦🐦	Fall	Chautauqua
🐦🐦	Fall	Chautauqua, Riverlands
🐦🐦🐦🐦	Fall	Chautauqua
🐦🐦🐦🐦	Fall	Chautauqua, Big Muddy (Cora Island)
🐦🐦🐦	Fall	Chautauqua and Emiquon
🐦🐦	Fall	Chautauqua and Sanganois

Order: Charadriiformes *(cntd.)*

Species	Rarity
Stilt Sandpiper (Calidris himantopus)	🐦🐦
Sanderling (Calidris alba)	🐦🐦🐦
Dunlin (Calidris alpina)	🐦🐦
Purple Sandpiper (Calidris maritima)	🐦🐦🐦🐦🐦
Baird's Sandpiper (Calidris bairdii)	🐦🐦
Least Sandpiper (Calidris minutilla)	🐦
White-rumped Sandpiper (Calidris fuscicollis)	🐦🐦
Buff-breasted Sandpiper (Calidris subruficollis)	🐦🐦🐦
Pectoral Sandpiper (Calidris melanotos)	🐦
Semipalmated Sandpiper (Calidris pusilla)	🐦
Western Sandpiper (Calidris mauri)	🐦🐦🐦
Short-billed Dowitcher (Limnodromus griseus)	🐦🐦
Long-billed Dowitcher (Limnodromus scolopaceus)	🐦🐦🐦
American Woodcock (Scolopax minor)	🐦🐦
Wilson's Snipe (Gallinago delicata)	🐦🐦
Spotted Sandpiper (Actitis macularius)	🐦
Solitary Sandpiper (Tringa solitaria)	🐦🐦
Lesser Yellowlegs (Tringa flavipes)	🐦
Willet (Tringa semipalmata)	🐦🐦🐦
Greater Yellowlegs (Tringa melanoleuca)	🐦
Wilson's Phalarope (Phalaropus tricolor)(endangered)	🐦🐦
Red-necked Phalarope (Phalaropus lobatus)	🐦🐦🐦
Red Phalarope (Phalaropus fulicarius)	🐦🐦🐦🐦

Family: Stercorariidae (Skuas and Jaegers)	Rarity
Pomarine Jaeger (Stercorarius pomarinus)	🐦🐦🐦🐦🐦
Parasitic Jaeger (Stercorarius parasiticus)	🐦🐦🐦🐦
Long-tailed Jaeger (Stercorarius longicaudus)	🐦🐦🐦🐦🐦

Family: Laridae (Gulls, Terns, and Skimmers)	
Black-legged Kittiwake (Rissa tridactyla)	🐦🐦🐦🐦🐦

Wow Factor	Best Season	Hot Spots
🐦🐦	Fall	Chautauqua, Riverlands
🐦	Fall	Chautauqua and Meredosia area
🐦🐦🐦	Fall	Chautauqua and Meredosia area
🐦🐦🐦	Fall	Any
🐦	Fall	Chautauqua, Riverlands
🐦	Fall	Chauatauqua, Riverlands
🐦🐦	Spring	Emiquon and Meredosia area
🐦🐦🐦	Fall	Chautauqua and Meredosia area
🐦🐦	Fall	Chautauqua, Ted and Pat Jones SP
🐦🐦	Fall	Chauatauqua, Riverlands
🐦🐦🐦	Fall	Chautauqua and Meredosia area
🐦🐦🐦	Spring	Meredosia area and Spunky bottoms
🐦🐦🐦	Fall	Chautauqua
🐦🐦🐦	Spring	Sand Ridge and Siloam Springs
🐦🐦	Any (Fall)	Any
🐦🐦	Spring	Any
🐦🐦	Fall	Chautauqua
🐦🐦	Fall	Chautauqua
🐦🐦🐦	Spring	Meredosia area and Spunky bottoms
🐦🐦	Fall	Chautauqua
🐦🐦🐦	Spring	Emiquon, Meredosia area and Spunky bottoms
🐦🐦🐦🐦	Fall	Chautauqua
🐦🐦🐦🐦	Fall	Chautauqua
Wow Factor	**Best Season**	**Hot Spots**
🐦🐦🐦🐦	Fall	Any
🐦🐦🐦🐦	Fall	Chautauqua and Emiquon
🐦🐦🐦🐦🐦	Fall	Chautauqua
🐦🐦🐦🐦	Winter	Any

Order: Charadriiformes *(cntd.)*

Ivory Gull (Pagophila eburnea)	🐦🐦🐦🐦🐦
Sabine's Gull (Xema sabini)	🐦🐦🐦🐦
Bonaparte's Gull (Chroicocephalus philadelphia)	🐦🐦
Little Gull (Hydrocoloeus minutus)	🐦🐦🐦🐦
Laughing Gull (Leucophaeus atricilla)	🐦🐦🐦
Franklin's Gull (Leucophaeus pipixcan)	🐦🐦
Ring-billed Gull (Larus delawarensis)	🐦
California Gull (Larus californicus)	🐦🐦🐦
Herring Gull (Larus argentatus)	🐦🐦
Iceland Gull (Larus glaucoides)	🐦🐦🐦
Lesser Black-backed Gull (Larus fuscus)	🐦🐦🐦
Glaucous-winged Gull (Larus glaucescens)	🐦🐦🐦🐦🐦
Glaucous Gull (Larus hyperboreus)	🐦🐦🐦
Great Black-backed Gull (Larus marinus)	🐦🐦🐦🐦
Least Tern (Sternula antillarum)(endangered)	🐦🐦🐦
Caspian Tern (Hydroprogne caspia)	🐦
Black Tern (Chlidonias niger) (endangered)	🐦🐦
Common Tern (Sterna hirundo) (endangered)	🐦🐦
Arctic Tern (Sterna paradisaea)	🐦🐦🐦🐦
Forster's Tern (Sterna forsteri) (endangered)	🐦
Royal Tern (Thalasseus maximus)	🐦🐦🐦🐦

Order: Gaviiformes

Family: Gaviidae (Loons)	Rarity
Red-throated Loon (Gavia stellata)	🐦🐦🐦
Pacific Loon (Gavia pacifica)	🐦🐦🐦🐦
Common Loon (Gavia immer)	🐦🐦

Wow Factor	Best Season	Hot Spots
🐦🐦🐦🐦🐦	Winter	Any
🐦🐦🐦🐦	Fall	Emiquon, Riverlands
🐦🐦🐦	Fall	Emiquon, Riverlands, Columbia Bottom
🐦🐦🐦	Spring	Jake Wolf fish hatchery
🐦🐦	Fall	Emiquon, Riverlands
🐦🐦🐦	Fall	Emiquon
🐦	Fall	Any
🐦	Winter	Peoria Lake, Riverlands, Two rivers NWR
🐦🐦	Winter	Peoria Lake
🐦🐦	Winter	Peoria Lake, Riverlands, Two rivers NWR
🐦🐦🐦	Winter	Peoria Lake
🐦🐦	Winter	Any
🐦🐦🐦	Winter	Peoria Lake
🐦🐦🐦	Winter	Peoria Lake
🐦🐦🐦	Spring	Meredosia area, Riverlands
🐦🐦	Summer	Emiquon
🐦🐦	Spring	Emiquon, Meredosia area, Two Rivers NWR
🐦🐦	Fall	Chautauqua and Emiquon
🐦🐦	Spring	Emiquon
🐦🐦	Spring	Emiquon
🐦🐦	Fall	Emiquon

Wow Factor	Best Season	Hot Spots
🐦🐦🐦	Fall	Emiquon
🐦🐦🐦	Fall	Emiquon
🐦🐦🐦🐦	Fall	Emquon and Peoria Lake, Lincoln Shields (Riverlands)

Order: Gaviiformes *(cntd.)*

Family: Phalacrocoracidae (Cormorants)	
Neotropic Cormorant (Phalacrocorax brasilianus) =	🐦🐦🐦
Double-crested Cormorant (Phalacrocorax auritus)	🐦

Order: Pelecaniformes

Family: Pelecanidae (Pelicans)	Rarity
American White Pelican (Pelecanus erythrorhynchos)	🐦
Brown Pelican (Pelecanus occidentalis)	🐦🐦🐦🐦

Family: Ardeidae (Bitterns, Herons, and Allies)	
American Bittern (Botaurus lentiginosus) (endangered)	🐦🐦
Least Bittern (Ixobrychus exilis) (threatened)	🐦🐦🐦
Great Blue Heron (Ardea herodias)	🐦
Great Egret (Ardea alba) (	🐦
Snowy Egret (Egretta thula) endangered)	🐦🐦
Little Blue Heron (Egretta caerulea) (endangered)	🐦🐦
Tricolored Heron (Egretta tricolor)	🐦🐦🐦🐦
Cattle Egret (Bubulcus ibis) (spec)	🐦🐦
Green Heron (Butorides virescens)	🐦🐦
Black-crowned Night-Heron (Nycticorax nycticorax) (endangered)	🐦🐦
Yellow-crowned Night-Heron (Nyctanassa violacea) (endangered)	🐦🐦🐦

Family: Threskiornithidae (Ibises and Spoonbills)	
White Ibis (Eudocimus albus)	🐦🐦🐦🐦
Glossy Ibis (Plegadis falcinellus)	🐦🐦🐦
White-faced Ibis (Plegadis chihi)	🐦🐦
Roseate Spoonbill (Platalea ajaja)	🐦🐦🐦🐦

Wow Factor	Best Season	Hot Spots
🐦🐦	Fall	Emiquon
🐦🐦	Fall	Any

Wow Factor	Best Season	Hot Spots
🐦🐦🐦	Fall	Chautauqua, Emiquon, Riverlands
🐦🐦🐦	Fall	Swan Lake

Wow Factor	Best Season	Hot Spots
🐦🐦🐦	Spring	Beardstown area and Emiquon
🐦🐦🐦	Spring	Beardstown area and Emiquon
🐦🐦	Any	Any
🐦	Any	Any
🐦🐦	Fall	Horseshoe Lake and Swan Lake
🐦🐦🐦	Fall	Horseshoe Lake and Swan Lake
🐦🐦🐦	Summer	Emiquon
🐦🐦🐦	Spring	Emiquon and Horeshoe Lake
🐦🐦	Spring	Any
🐦🐦🐦	Spring	Emiquon, Horeshoe Lake, Big Muddy NWR (Cora Island)
🐦🐦🐦	Fall	Cahokia Mounds

Wow Factor	Best Season	Hot Spots
🐦🐦🐦	Fall	Horseshoe Lake
🐦🐦🐦	Spring	Emiquon, Riverlands
🐦🐦🐦	Spring	Emiquon and Meredosia area
🐦🐦🐦🐦🐦	Fall	Any

Order: Cathartiformes

Family: Cathartidae (New World Vultures)	Rarity
Black Vulture (Coragyps atratus)	🐦🐦🐦🐦
Turkey Vulture (Cathartes aura)	🐦

Order: Accipitriformes

Family: Pandionidae (Ospreys)	Rarity
Osprey (Pandion haliaetus)(endangered)	🐦🐦

Family: Accipitridae (Hawks, Kites, Eagles, and Allies)	Rarity
Swallow-tailed Kite (Elanoides forficatus)	🐦🐦🐦🐦
Mississippi Kite (Ictinia mississippiensis) (threatened)	🐦🐦
Bald Eagle (Haliaeetus leucocephalus)	🐦
Northern Harrier (Circus hudsonius) (endangered)	🐦
Sharp-shinned Hawk (Accipiter striatus)	🐦
Cooper's Hawk (Accipiter cooperii)	🐦
Northern Goshawk (Accipiter gentilis)	🐦🐦🐦🐦
Red-shouldered Hawk (Buteo lineatus)	🐦🐦
Broad-winged Hawk (Buteo platypterus)	🐦🐦
Swainson's Hawk (Buteo swainsoni) (endangered)	🐦🐦🐦
Red-tailed Hawk (Buteo jamaicensis)	🐦
Rough-legged Hawk (Buteo lagopus)	🐦🐦
Golden Eagle (Aquila chrysaetos)	🐦🐦

Order: Strigiformes

Family: Tytonidae (Barn Owls)	Rarity
Barn Owl (Tyto alba) (threatened)	🐦🐦🐦

Wow Factor	Best Season	Hot Spots
🐦	Any	Anywhere south of St Louis
🐦	Any	Any

Wow Factor	Best Season	Hot Spots
🐦🐦🐦	Summer	Chautauqua and Banner Marsh
🐦🐦🐦	Fall	Any
🐦🐦🐦	Summer	Stump Lake , Columbia Bottom
🐦🐦🐦	Winter	Riverlands north to Two Rivers NWR
🐦🐦	Winter	Emiquon and Meredosia area
🐦🐦	Winter	Any
🐦🐦	Any	Any
🐦🐦🐦🐦	Winter	Sand Ridge
🐦🐦	Any	Stump Lake
🐦🐦	Fall	Siloam Springs
🐦🐦	Spring	Meredosia area
🐦	Any	Any
🐦🐦🐦	Winter	Spunky Bottoms area and Emiquon
🐦🐦🐦	Winter	Stump Lake and Big Lake

Wow Factor	Best Season	Hot Spots
🐦🐦🐦	Any	Anywhere with nest boxes

Order: Strigiformes *(cntd.)*

Family: Strigidae (Typical Owls)	
Eastern Screech-Owl (Megascops asio)	🐦🐦
Great Horned Owl (Bubo virginianus)	🐦
Snowy Owl (Bubo scandiacus)	🐦🐦🐦
Burrowing Owl (Athene cunicularia)	🐦🐦🐦🐦
Barred Owl (Strix varia)	🐦
Long-eared Owl (Asio otus)	🐦🐦
Short-eared Owl (Asio flammeus) (endangered)	🐦
Northern Saw-whet Owl (Aegolius acadicus)	🐦🐦

Order: Coraciiformes

Family: Alcedinidae (Kingfishers)	Rarity
Belted Kingfisher (Megaceryle alcyon)	🐦

Order: Piciformes

Family: Picidae (Woodpeckers and Allies)	Rarity
Red-headed Woodpecker (Melanerpes erythrocephalus)	🐦
Red-bellied Woodpecker (Melanerpes carolinus)	🐦
Yellow-bellied Sapsucker (Sphyrapicus varius)	🐦
Downy Woodpecker (Picoides pubescens)	🐦
Hairy Woodpecker (Picoides villosus)	🐦🐦
Northern Flicker (Colaptes auratus)	🐦
Pileated Woodpecker (Dryocopus pileatus)	🐦🐦

Wow Factor	Best Season	Hot Spots
(2 birds)	Any	Sand Ridge
(4 birds)	Any	Meredosia area
(5 birds)	Winter	Anywhere in an irruption year
(3 birds)	Spring	Any
(2 birds)	Any	Sand Ridge
(4 birds)	Winter	Any cedar groove
(4 birds)	Winter	Meredosia, Riverlands (at twilight)
(4 birds)	Winter	Sand Ridge

Wow Factor	Best Season	Hot Spots
(2 birds)	Any	Any

Wow Factor	Best Season	Hot Spots
(4 birds)	Summer	Areas south of Havana and Chautauqua
(2 birds)	Any	Any
(3 birds)	Winter	Sand Ridge
(3 birds)	Any	Any
(3 birds)	Any	Any
(3 birds)	Any	Any
(4 birds)	Any	Sand Ridge

Order: Falconiformes

Family: Falconidae (Caracaras and Falcons)	Rarity
American Kestrel (Falco sparverius)	🐦
Merlin (Falco columbarius)	🐦🐦
Peregrine Falcon (Falco peregrinus)	🐦🐦
Prairie Falcon (Falco mexicanus)	🐦🐦🐦🐦

Order: Passeriformes

Family: Tyrannidae (Tyrant Flycatchers)	Rarity
Olive-sided Flycatcher (Contopus cooperi)	🐦🐦
Eastern Wood-Pewee (Contopus virens)	🐦
Yellow-bellied Flycatcher (Empidonax flaviventris)	🐦🐦
Acadian Flycatcher (Empidonax virescens)	🐦
Alder Flycatcher (Empidonax alnorum)	🐦🐦
Willow Flycatcher (Empidonax traillii)	🐦
Least Flycatcher (Empidonax minimus)	🐦
Eastern Phoebe (Sayornis phoebe)	🐦
Say's Phoebe (Sayornis saya)	🐦🐦🐦🐦
Great Crested Flycatcher (Myiarchus crinitus)	🐦
Western Kingbird (Tyrannus verticalis)	🐦🐦
Eastern Kingbird (Tyrannus tyrannus)	🐦
Scissor-tailed Flycatcher (Tyrannus forficatus)	🐦🐦🐦
Fork-tailed Flycatcher (Tyrannus savana)	🐦🐦🐦🐦🐦
Family: Laniidae (Shrikes)	
Loggerhead Shrike (Lanius ludovicianus) (endangered)	🐦🐦
Northern Shrike (Lanius borealis)	🐦🐦

Wow Factor	Best Season	Hot Spots
🐦🐦🐦	Any	Any
🐦🐦	Fall	Ted and Pat Jones State Park
🐦🐦🐦🐦	Fall	Chautauqua
🐦🐦🐦	Winter	Spunky Bottoms area

Wow Factor	Best Season	Hot Spots
🐦🐦🐦	Spring	Sand Ridge, Riverlands (Ellis Island)
🐦🐦	Summer	Siloam Springs
🐦🐦🐦	Spring	Sand Ridge
🐦🐦	Summer	Siloam Springs, Riverlands (Ellis Island)
🐦🐦	Spring	Sand Ridge, Riverlands (Ellis Island)
🐦🐦	Summer	Emiquon
🐦🐦	Spring	Sand Ridge
🐦🐦	Spring	Any
🐦🐦🐦	Fall	Any
🐦🐦🐦	Spring	Siloam Springs, Riverlands (Ellis Island)
🐦🐦🐦	Summer	Areas south of Havana, Meredosia area, and East St. Louis
🐦🐦	Spring	Any
🐦🐦🐦🐦🐦	Summer	Areas south of Havana
🐦🐦🐦🐦🐦	Fall	Any
🐦🐦	Winter	Any
🐦🐦		Jim Edger and Sanganois

Order: Passeriformes *(cntd.)*

Family: Vireonidae (Vireos)	
White-eyed Vireo (Vireo griseus)	
Bell's Vireo (Vireo bellii)	
Yellow-throated Vireo (Vireo flavifrons)	
Blue-headed Vireo (Vireo solitarius)	
Philadelphia Vireo (Vireo philadelphicus)	
Warbling Vireo (Vireo gilvus)	
Red-eyed Vireo (Vireo olivaceus)	
Family: Corvidae (Crows and Jays)	
Blue Jay (Cyanocitta cristata)	
American Crow (Corvus brachyrhynchos)	
Fish Crow (Corvus ossifragus)	
Family: Alaudidae (Larks)	
Horned Lark (Eremophila alpestris)	
Family: Hirundinidae (Swallows)	
Purple Martin (Progne subis)	
Tree Swallow (Tachycineta bicolor)	
Northern Rough-winged Swallow (Stelgidopteryx serripennis)	
Bank Swallow (Riparia riparia)	
Cliff Swallow (Petrochelidon pyrrhonota)	
Cave Swallow (Petrochelidon fulva)	
Barn Swallow (Hirundo rustica)	
Family: Paridae (Chickadees and Titmice)	
Carolina Chickadee (Poecile carolinensis)	
Black-capped Chickadee (Poecile atricapillus)	

Birds	Season	Location
🐦🐦🐦	Spring	Copperhead Hallow
🐦🐦	Summer	Emiquon
🐦🐦🐦🐦	Spring	Siloam Springs
🐦🐦🐦🐦	Fall	Sand Ridge
🐦🐦🐦	Fall	Chautauqua, Riverlands (Ellis Island)
🐦🐦	Summer	Any
🐦🐦	Spring	Siloam Springs
🐦🐦	Any	Any
🐦	Any	Any
🐦🐦	Spring	Stump Lake, Pere Marquette, Riverlands, Two Rivers NWR
🐦🐦	Any	Any
🐦🐦🐦	Spring	Any
🐦🐦	Fall	Any
🐦🐦	Fall	Any
🐦🐦	Fall	Two Rivers NWR
🐦🐦🐦	Spring	Emiquon
🐦🐦🐦🐦	Fall	Any
🐦🐦	Spring	Any
🐦🐦🐦	Any	Horeshoe Lake
🐦🐦🐦	Any	Any

Order: Passeriformes *(cntd.)*

Tufted Titmouse (Baeolophus bicolor)	

Family: Sittidae **(Nuthatches)**	
Red-breasted Nuthatch (Sitta canadensis)	
White-breasted Nuthatch (Sitta carolinensis)	

Family: Certhiidae **(Creepers)**	
Brown Creeper (Certhia americana)	

Family: Troglodytidae **(Wrens)**	
Rock Wren (Salpinctes obsoletus)	
House Wren (Troglodytes aedon)	
Winter Wren (Troglodytes hiemalis)	
Sedge Wren (Cistothorus platensis)	
Marsh Wren (Cistothorus palustris)	
Carolina Wren (Thryothorus ludovicianus)	
Bewick's Wren (Thryomanes bewickii) (endangered)	

Family: Polioptilidae **(Gnatcatchers and Gnatwrens)**	
Blue-gray Gnatcatcher (Polioptila caerulea)	

Family: Regulidae **(Kinglets)**	
Golden-crowned Kinglet (Regulus satrapa)	
Ruby-crowned Kinglet (Regulus calendula)	

Family: Turdidae **(Thrushes)**	
Eastern Bluebird (Sialia sialis)	
Veery (Catharus fuscescens)	

🐦🐦	Any	Any
🐦🐦🐦	Fall	Sand ridge
🐦🐦🐦	Any	Any
🐦🐦	Winter	Any
🐦🐦🐦	Winter	Riverlands
🐦🐦	Summer	Any
🐦🐦🐦	Fall	Sanganois
🐦🐦	Summer	Emiquon
🐦🐦	Spring	Bearstown Marsh
🐦🐦🐦	Any	Any
🐦🐦🐦	Spring	Siloam Springs
🐦🐦🐦🐦	Spring	Any
🐦🐦🐦	Winter	Sand Ridge
🐦🐦🐦	Fall	Sand Ridge
🐦🐦🐦🐦	Any	Spunky Bottoms area, Columbia Bottom
🐦🐦	Spring	Sand Ridge, Columbia Bottom

Order: Passeriformes *(cntd.)*

Gray-cheeked Thrush (Catharus minimus)	🐦🐦
Swainson's Thrush (Catharus ustulatus)	🐦
Hermit Thrush (Catharus guttatus)	🐦🐦
Wood Thrush (Hylocichla mustelina)	🐦
American Robin (Turdus migratorius)	🐦
Varied Thrush (Ixoreus naevius)	🐦🐦🐦🐦🐦

Family: Mimidae
(Mockingbirds and Thrashers)

Gray Catbird (Dumetella carolinensis)	🐦
Brown Thrasher (Toxostoma rufum)	🐦
Northern Mockingbird (Mimus polyglottos)	🐦

Family: Sturnidae
(Starlings)

European Starling (Sturnus vulgaris)	🐦

Family: Bombycillidae
(Waxwings)

Cedar Waxwing (Bombycilla cedrorum)	🐦

Family: Passeridae
(Old World Sparrows)

House Sparrow (Passer domesticus)	🐦
Eurasian Tree Sparrow (Passer montanus)	🐦

Family: Motacillidae
(Wagtails and Pipits)

American Pipit (Anthus rubescens)	🐦
Sprague's Pipit (Anthus spragueii)	🐦🐦🐦🐦

🐦🐦	Spring	Sand Ridge
🐦🐦	Fall	Sand Ridge
🐦🐦	Winter	Sand Ridge, Columbia Bottom
🐦🐦🐦	Spring	Siloam Springs
🐦🐦	Any	Any
🐦🐦🐦🐦	Winter	Any
🐦🐦	Spring	Any
🐦🐦	Spring	Any
🐦🐦🐦	Summer	Areas south of Havana
🐦🐦	Any	Any
🐦🐦🐦	Spring	Sand Ridge
🐦	Any	Any
🐦🐦	Any	Chautuauqa, Riverlands
🐦🐦	Fall	Emiquon, Columbia Bottom
🐦🐦🐦	Spring	Any

Order: Passeriformes *(cntd.)*

Family: Fringillidae (Fringilline and Cardueline Finches and Allies)	
Evening Grosbeak (Coccothraustes vespertinus)	🐦🐦🐦🐦
Pine Grosbeak (Pinicola enucleator)	🐦🐦🐦🐦
House Finch (Haemorhous mexicanus)	🐦
Purple Finch (Haemorhous purpureus)	🐦🐦
Common Redpoll (Acanthis flammea)	🐦🐦🐦
Red Crossbill (Loxia curvirostra)	🐦🐦🐦
White-winged Crossbill (Loxia leucoptera)	🐦🐦🐦🐦
Pine Siskin (Spinus pinus)	🐦🐦
American Goldfinch (Spinus tristis)	🐦
Family: Calcariidae (Longspurs and Snow Bunting)	
Lapland Longspur (Calcarius lapponicus)	🐦
Smith's Longspur (Calcarius pictus)	🐦🐦
Snow Bunting (Plectrophenax nivalis)	🐦🐦
Family: Passerellidae (New World Sparrows)	
Spotted Towhee (Pipilo maculatus)	🐦🐦🐦
Eastern Towhee (Pipilo erythrophthalmus)	🐦
American Tree Sparrow (Spizelloides arborea)	🐦
Chipping Sparrow (Spizella passerina)	🐦
Clay-colored Sparrow (Spizella pallida)	🐦🐦🐦
Field Sparrow (Spizella pusilla)	🐦
Vesper Sparrow (Pooecetes gramineus)	🐦🐦
Lark Sparrow (Chondestes grammacus)	🐦🐦
Savannah Sparrow (Passerculus sandwichensis)	🐦
Grasshopper Sparrow (Ammodramus savannarum)	🐦🐦

🐦🐦🐦🐦	Winter	Sand Ridge
🐦🐦🐦🐦	Winter	Sand Ridge
🐦🐦	Any	Any
🐦🐦🐦	Winter	Sand Ridge
🐦🐦🐦	Winter	Chautauqua and Big Lake
🐦🐦🐦🐦	Winter	Sand Ridge
🐦🐦🐦🐦	Winter	Sand Ridge
🐦🐦	Winter	Sand Ridge
🐦🐦🐦🐦	Any	Any
🐦🐦	Winter	Spunky Bottoms area
🐦🐦🐦	Spring	Emiquon and Spunky Bottomas area
🐦🐦🐦	Winter	Emiquon and Spunky Bottomas area
🐦🐦🐦	Winter	Spunky Bottoms area
🐦🐦	Any	Siloam Springs
🐦🐦	Winter	Riverlands
🐦🐦	Spring	Any
🐦🐦🐦	Fall	Emiquon, Big Muddy NWR (Cora Island)
🐦🐦	Spring	Siloam Springs, Big Muddy NWR (Cora Island)
🐦🐦	Spring	Meredosia Area, Big Muddy NWR (Cora Island)
🐦🐦🐦	Summer	Areas south of Havana
🐦🐦	Fall	Any
🐦🐦🐦	Spring	Meredosia area zand areas south of Havana

Order: Passeriformes *(cntd.)*

Henslow's Sparrow (Ammodramus henslowii)	🐦🐦
LeConte's Sparrow (Ammodramus leconteii)	🐦🐦
Nelson's Sparrow (Ammodramus nelsoni)	🐦🐦🐦
Fox Sparrow (Passerella iliaca)	🐦🐦
Song Sparrow (Melospiza melodia)	🐦
Lincoln's Sparrow (Melospiza lincolnii)	🐦🐦
Swamp Sparrow (Melospiza georgiana)	🐦
White-throated Sparrow (Zonotrichia albicollis)	🐦
Harris's Sparrow (Zonotrichia querula)	🐦🐦🐦
White-crowned Sparrow (Zonotrichia leucophrys)	🐦
Dark-eyed Junco (Junco hyemalis)	🐦

Family: Icteriidae (Yellow-breasted Chats)	
Yellow-breasted Chat (Icteria virens)	🐦

Family: Icteridae (Blackbirds)	
Yellow-headed Blackbird (Xanthocephalus xanthocephalus) (endangered)	🐦🐦🐦
Bobolink (Dolichonyx oryzivorus)	🐦🐦
Eastern Meadowlark (Sturnella magna)	🐦
Western Meadowlark (Sturnella neglecta)	🐦🐦
Orchard Oriole (Icterus spurius)	🐦
Baltimore Oriole (Icterus galbula)	🐦
Red-winged Blackbird (Agelaius phoeniceus)	🐦
Brown-headed Cowbird (Molothrus ater)	🐦
Rusty Blackbird (Euphagus carolinus)	🐦🐦🐦
Brewer's Blackbird (Euphagus cyanocephalus)	🐦🐦
Common Grackle (Quiscalus quiscula)	🐦

🐦🐦🐦	Summer	Siloam Springs and Emiquon
🐦🐦🐦	Fall	Emiquon, Big Muddy NWR (Cora
🐦🐦🐦	Fall	Island)
		Emiquon
🐦🐦	Fall	Sand Ridge
🐦🐦	Any	Any
🐦🐦🐦	Fall	Emiquon and Meredosia area
🐦🐦	Fall	Emiquon and Beardstown marsh
🐦🐦	Fall	Any
🐦🐦🐦	Fall	Emiquon and Spunky Bottoms area
🐦🐦	Fall	Any
🐦🐦	Winter	Any
🐦🐦🐦	Spring	Siloam Springs
🐦🐦🐦🐦🐦	Spring	Emiquon and Meredosia area
🐦🐦🐦🐦	Fall	Emiquon and Big Lake
🐦🐦	Any	Any
🐦🐦🐦	Spring	Meredosia area, Big Muddy NWR (Cora Island)
🐦🐦🐦	Spring	Emiquon, Ted and Pat Jones State Park
🐦🐦🐦	Spring	Siloam Springs
🐦	Any	Any
🐦	Any	Any
🐦🐦	Fall	Meredosia area
🐦🐦	Fall	Emiquon
🐦🐦	Any	Any

Order: Passeriformes *(cntd.)*

Family: Parulidae (Wood-Warblers)	Rarity
Ovenbird (Seiurus aurocapilla)	🐦
Worm-eating Warbler (Helmitheros vermivorum)	🐦🐦🐦
Louisiana Waterthrush (Parkesia motacilla)	🐦
Northern Waterthrush (Parkesia noveboracensis)	🐦
Golden-winged Warbler (Vermivora chrysoptera)	🐦🐦
Blue-winged Warbler (Vermivora cyanoptera)	🐦🐦🐦
Black-and-white Warbler (Mniotilta varia)	🐦
Prothonotary Warbler (Protonotaria citrea)	🐦
Swainson's Warbler (Limnothlypis swainsonii) (endangered)	🐦🐦🐦🐦
Tennessee Warbler (Oreothlypis peregrina)	🐦🐦
Orange-crowned Warbler (Oreothlypis celata)	🐦🐦
Nashville Warbler (Oreothlypis ruficapilla)	🐦
Connecticut Warbler (Oporornis agilis)	🐦🐦🐦
Mourning Warbler (Geothlypis philadelphia)	🐦🐦
Kentucky Warbler (Geothlypis formosa)	🐦
Common Yellowthroat (Geothlypis trichas)	🐦
Hooded Warbler (Setophaga citrina)	🐦
American Redstart (Setophaga ruticilla)	🐦
Kirtland's Warbler (Setophaga kirtlandii)	🐦🐦🐦🐦🐦
Cape May Warbler (Setophaga tigrina)	🐦🐦
Cerulean Warbler (Setophaga cerulea) (threatened)	🐦🐦
Northern Parula (Setophaga americana)	🐦
Magnolia Warbler (Setophaga magnolia)	🐦
Bay-breasted Warbler (Setophaga castanea)	🐦🐦🐦
Blackburnian Warbler (Setophaga fusca)	🐦🐦🐦
Yellow Warbler (Setophaga petechia)	🐦
Chestnut-sided Warbler (Setophaga pensylvanica)	🐦
Blackpoll Warbler (Setophaga striata)	🐦🐦
Black-throated Blue Warbler (Setophaga caerulescens)	🐦🐦🐦

Wow Factor	Best Season	Hot Spots
🐦🐦🐦	Spring	Copperhead Hallow
🐦🐦🐦	Spring	Pere Marquette and Siloam Springs
🐦🐦	Spring	Pere Marquette and Siloam Springs
🐦🐦	Spring	Spunky Bottoms area
🐦🐦🐦🐦🐦	Spring	Sand Ridge
🐦🐦🐦🐦🐦	Spring	Siloam Springs
🐦🐦🐦🐦🐦	Spring	Sand RIdge
🐦🐦🐦🐦🐦	Summer	Stump Lake and Meredosia area
🐦🐦🐦	Spring	Any
🐦🐦🐦🐦	Spring	Sand Ridge,Riverlands (Ellis Island)
🐦🐦	Fall	Meredosia area
🐦🐦🐦	Spring	Sand Ridge
🐦🐦🐦🐦	Spring	Sand Ridge
🐦🐦🐦🐦	Spring	Sand Ridge, Riverlands (Ellis Island)
🐦🐦🐦🐦	Spring	Siloam Springs
🐦🐦🐦	Spring	Emiquon
🐦🐦🐦🐦🐦	Spring	Copperhead Hallow and Pere Marquette
🐦🐦🐦🐦	Spring	Sanganois
🐦🐦🐦🐦	Spring	Any
🐦🐦🐦🐦	Spring	Sand Ridge
🐦🐦🐦🐦🐦	Spring	Pere Marquette and Siloam Springs
🐦🐦🐦🐦🐦	Spring	Pere Marquette and Siloam Springs
🐦🐦🐦🐦	Spring	Sand Ridge
🐦🐦🐦🐦	Fall	Sand Ridge
🐦🐦🐦🐦🐦	Fall	Sand Ridge
🐦🐦🐦	Spring	Siloam Springs
🐦🐦🐦🐦	Spring	Sand Ridge
🐦🐦🐦🐦	Spring	Sand Ridge, Columbia Bottom
🐦🐦🐦🐦	Fall	Chautauqua

Order: Passeriformes *(cntd.)*

Palm Warbler (Setophaga palmarum)	🪶
Pine Warbler (Setophaga pinus)	🪶
Yellow-rumped Warbler (Setophaga coronata)	🪶
Yellow-throated Warbler (Setophaga dominica)	🪶🪶
Prairie Warbler (Setophaga discolor)	🪶🪶
Black-throated Gray Warbler (Setophaga nigrescens)	🪶🪶🪶🪶🪶
Townsend's Warbler (Setophaga townsendi)	🪶🪶🪶🪶🪶
Black-throated Green Warbler (Setophaga virens)	🪶🪶
Canada Warbler (Cardellina canadensis)	🪶🪶
Wilson's Warbler (Cardellina pusilla)	🪶🪶
Family: Cardinalidae (Cardinals and Allies)	
Summer Tanager (Piranga rubra)	🪶
Scarlet Tanager (Piranga olivacea)	🪶
Northern Cardinal (Cardinalis cardinalis)	🪶
Rose-breasted Grosbeak (Pheucticus ludovicianus)	🪶
Blue Grosbeak (Passerina caerulea)	🪶
Indigo Bunting (Passerina cyanea)	🪶
Painted Bunting (Passerina ciris)	🪶🪶🪶
Dickcissel (Spiza americana)	🪶

🐦🐦	Spring	Chautauqua
🐦🐦🐦	Spring	Sand Ridge
🐦🐦🐦	Spring	Meredosia area
🐦🐦🐦	Spring	Copperhead Hallow
🐦🐦🐦🐦	Spring	Siloam Springs, Columbia Bottom
🐦🐦🐦	Spring	Any
🐦🐦🐦🐦	Spring	Any
🐦🐦🐦🐦	Spring	Sand ridge
🐦🐦🐦🐦	Spring	Sand Ridge
🐦🐦🐦	Spring	Sand Ridge, Columbia Bottom
🐦🐦🐦🐦	Spring	Siloam Springs
🐦🐦🐦🐦🐦	Spring	Sand Ridge
🐦🐦🐦	Any	Any
🐦🐦🐦🐦	Fall	Sand Ridge
🐦🐦🐦🐦	Spring	Meredosia area, Columbia Bottom, Riverlands
🐦🐦🐦🐦	Spring	Any
🐦🐦🐦🐦🐦	Summer	East St. Louis
🐦🐦	Summer	Meredosia area

ABOUT THE AUTHORS

Dr. Joe Steensma is a professor at Washington University in St. Louis, Missouri. He has been birding along the Illinois River for more than twenty years, but his abnormal addiction to bird-watching started long before that. An owl devouring a squirrel in the winter of 1977 got him hooked and there was no turning back. He continues to conduct bird surveys in the Midwest, the Bahamas, Australia, and Costa Rica. He is the author of many peer-reviewed scientific articles as well as "A Guide to the Birds of North Andros Island".

Colin Dobson started birding at the ripe old age of 7 years. A bit of a late bloomer, he has made up for lost time by logging thousands of hours in the field over the past decade. He is widely known throughout the region as being one of the most prolific birdwatchers in Illinois. He has recorded 365 species in the state of Illinois and over 330 in the Illinois River Flyway region. His notes are considered to be some of the most comprehensive records of the region over the past decade. Colin will graduate from high school in 2019.

42012678R00080

Made in the USA
Middletown, DE
15 April 2019